PEACEFAKERS, PEACEBREAKERS, *and* PEACEMAKERS

KEN SANDE
& KAY MOORE

HANNIBAL BOOKS
www.hannibalbooks.com

To order copies of
Peacefakers,
Peacebreakers, and
Peacemakers
Leader Guide, Member Book, Video,
Trade Book and Leader Kit
see order form in back of Member Book

or contact:
Hannibal Books
P.O. Box 461592
Garland, Texas 75046
Fax: 1-972-487-7960
Phone: 1-800-747-0738
Email: *hannibalbooks@earthlink.net*
Visit: *www.hannibalbooks.com*

Library of Congress Control Number: 2004111001
ISBN 0-929292-94-4

TABLE OF CONTENTS

4

INTRODUCTION

Peacefakers, Peacebreakers, and Peacemakers is a Bible study designed to be used in a Sunday-school class setting to help members learn life-changing principles of conflict resolution. This *Leader Guide* provides step-by-step guidance for leading group sessions in each week's study. By studying this *Guide,* you will learn how to best teach your group members and encourage peacemaking in their lives.

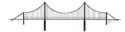

The Process of
Peacefakers, Peacebreakers, and Peacemakers

Peacefakers, Peacebreakers, and Peacemakers employs an interactive learning process. Members gather for group sessions during the Sunday-school time frame of their church. As the leader presents the material and guides the discussion, members share ways they are growing in their ability to understand biblical concepts of peacemaking; others give feedback and are encouraged in their own challenges and victories.

Churches may choose to present a six-week or a 12-week course. The first six weeks will provide members with a basic knowledge of the biblical principles of conflict resolution. If members want to delve more deeply into this subject, the class may choose to continue into the second six weeks of material and the group sessions supporting it.

Although each session stands on its own and is not a prerequisite for the one to follow, members benefit far more from attending all sessions and allowing the information received one week to build on the previous week's information.

Some members will desire to participate in a group study-ing *Peacefakers, Peacebreakers, and Peacemakers* because they have had a positive experience in reading *The Peacemaker* by Ken Sande. (This material—*Peacefakers, Peacebreakers, and Peacemakers*—is based on the third edition of *The Peacemaker*.) Churches and individuals throughout the world have used *The Peacemaker* to learn biblical concepts of peacemaking. However, reading *The Peacemaker* is not a prerequisite for this course. Members will benefit from *Peacefakers, Peacebreakers, and Peacemakers* even if they have not read *The Peacemaker*. Taking this study first, before one has read *The Peacemaker*, is perfectly acceptable. The group process of *Peacefakers, Peacebreakers, and Peacemakers* will introduce members to key peacemaking concepts and will help them to think more deeply than they would on their own. (Members will be assigned certain sections of *The Peacemaker* to read as part of optional, further study in this course.)

Steps for Offering *Peacefakers, Peacebreakers, and Peacemakers* in Your Church

1. *Pray.* Seek God's direction in determining whether a study of *Peacefakers, Peacebreakers, and Peacemakers* is appropriate for your church or for your individual Sunday-school class.
2. *Seek approval.* If you are a church-staff member, discuss your proposal with your pastor, or whoever guides the approval process in your church. If you are a Sunday-school teacher or church member, consult your pastor, an appropriate church-staff member, or the director of your Sunday-school department (if applicable) before you schedule a study of this resource. Provide the pastor or other church leaders with a copy of the *Member Book*, this *Leader Guide*, the accompanying video, and perhaps the

book, *The Peacemaker.* Help church leaders understand the process, goals, content, and procedures.

3. *Select leaders and provide training.* If you are a church-staff member or church leader who envisions offering this study of *Peacefakers, Peacebreakers, and Peacemakers* to several Sunday-school classes at a time, in a church-wide study or partial church-wide study, use the section, "How to Train Leaders" on page 13, to train persons to lead *The Peacefakers, Peacebreakers, and Peacemakers* groups. Refer to the section "Who can lead a group in *Peacefakers, Peacebreakers, and Peacemakers?*" on page 9 as you recruit persons to lead.

4. *Set a date for groups to begin.* The six-week format of each of the two parts of *Peacefakers, Peacebreakers, and Peacemakers* lends itself to a wide variety of usages. It can be used, for example, to kick off a church's Sunday-school year, which many churches observe during the fall or at back-to-school time. It is ideal for a study during the summer, when churches may switch gears from their traditional fall-to-spring studies. *Peacefakers, Peacebreakers, and Peacemakers* is also designed to be used in formats other than the traditional Sunday-school time frame on Sunday mornings. Other usages for this study may occur in men's or women's weekday Bible studies, discipleship courses, missions groups, or other church programs. Studying the two six-week units back-to-back is the ideal way to offer *Peacefakers, Peacebreakers, and Peacemakers.* However, a church could offer Part 1 (the first six weeks) in the fall and Part 2 (the second six weeks) in the spring without members being significantly deprived of the momentum that builds in a sequential study.

5. *Promote the study.* Schedule at least a four-week period to promote the study in your church. Place announcements in church publications and on bulletin boards; make announcements in worship services, Bible-study classes, discipleship groups, and women's and men's groups. Nothing would add appeal to this class as much as would a strong endorsement from your pastor.

6. *Organize groups.* This material may be taught to classes

organized by age, marital status, or stage in life (such as parents of young children), to name a few groups. However, a church may desire to offer a study of *Peacefakers, Peacebreakers, and Peacemakers* as part of a special emphasis in which a variety of ages and life circumstances are blended. This situation can be beneficial because members can learn from each others' experiences. Young professionals can learn from retirees, while newlyweds can inspire long-term marrieds, and so on. *Peacefakers, Peacebreakers, and Peacemakers* is designed to work well with mixed ages, mixed genders, and mixed life circumstances (for example, parents of preschoolers along with retirees), as well as with strictly age-graded groups.

7. *Order materials.* At least six weeks before the starting date, order one *Member Book* for each participant. If a couple participates, order individual books for both husband and wife. Be certain to order a *Member Book* for the leader. *Peacefakers, Peacebreakers, and Peacemakers* resources include

• *Peacefakers, Peacebreakers, and Peacemakers Member Book* (ISBN 0-929292-95-2)

• *Peacefakers, Peacebreakers, and Peacemakers Leader Kit* (ISBN 0-929292-99-5—*Member Book, Leader Guide*, and video)

8. *Set fees.* Asking members to pay at least part of the cost of their *Peacefakers, Peacebreakers, and Peacemakers Member Book* is usually wise. A person normally has more emotional investment to a study if he or she has covered at least part of the cost. Since cost may be a barrier to some people, however, offering scholarships to those who need them is helpful.

9. *Get started.* Read the *Leader Guide* and complete the member material yourself before you attempt to lead the study. Work at least one week ahead of the group you lead. For example, before you conduct group session 1, be sure you have studied not only week 1 but also week 2, completed your own *Member Book*, and watched the corresponding video segments, so that you can give members any special instructions necessary for the following week.

How to Lead a Group in *Peacefakers, Peacebreakers, and Peacemakers*

1. *Who can lead a group in* Peacefakers, Peacebreakers, and Peacemakers? Any mature Christian, either a layperson or church leader, can lead the group. The group leader may be the designated Sunday-school teacher for a class that has elected to study the material, or the class may prefer to designate one of its members or to enlist an outside leader for this particular study. A person may resist leading a group because he or she thinks, *I'm still struggling in the area of peacemaking. I strive to be a peacemaking Christian, but I'm not there yet.* In reality, the ideal leader is a fellow struggler—someone who relates to the issues involved and who is perhaps just a little farther down the road than the rest of his or her group members in terms of surrendering every aspect of his or her life to God's control. An ideal leader is someone who has struggled with making peace God's way and who can transparently share from his or her own personal experiences. Because the group leader teaches best by modeling, recruiting leaders who are role models in terms of living biblical peacemaking principles is important. Assure leaders whom you recruit that this *Leader Guide* provides ample, detailed instructions on how to lead the group. It is recommended, though not required, that a leader read the third edition of *The Peacemaker* before the person leads *Peacefakers, Peacebreakers, and Peacemakers.*

2. *What are some traits of an effective group leader?* This person has the following qualities:
- Is a growing Christian, a person of prayer, and someone who has faith in God's goodness and power;
- Is an active member of the sponsoring church;
- Has a commitment to keep confidential information private;
- Is an active member of the sponsoring church;
- Relates well to people;

- Has a solid knowledge of Scripture;
- Senses God's call to be involved in a ministry of helping others learn how to be biblical peacemakers;
- Is comfortable in the presence of people who share painful life experiences. In the process of these group discussions, members may reflect on hurtful times when they have responded improperly to conflict situations or other wrong choices they have made when relating to God or others. A person who feels comfortable only when those around him or her are cheerful and upbeat may need to reconsider whether he or she is the appropriate person to lead a group in *Peacefakers, Peacebreakers, and Peacemakers.*

3. *What are some skills that a group leader needs?*

A successful group leader will use the following group-leadership techniques:

- Maintain eye contact as members share. When appropriate, nod your head or use occasional verbal phrases to indicate that you are listening.
- Use good listening skills. To encourage sharing, make sure you or another member offers some type of response when any group member shares. Otherwise the person might feel embarrassed and say no more.
- Try to read body language and nonverbal cues. Attempt to draw out people who seem to be listening intently, withdrawing, or looking as though they are full of pain. Ask God for sensitivity.
- Affirm strong emotions such as tears. Phrases such as, "I sense the hurt in what you just shared" or "I'm sure that must be disappointing" help members identify their emotions and validate them.
- Avoid allowing one member to dominate discussions. If someone has talked too long, gently try to steer the conversation to someone else. Help the person summarize. Watch for the slightest break in a monologue to turn the conversation to someone else. State, "I'm wondering whether anyone else has a thought to share on this."

- Steer the group away from giving assertive advice. Help members share their own experiences ("Something that has worked for me is . . ." or "Here's what I've learned . . ." instead of "What you should do is . . .").

4. *What is an effective room arrangement?*

Use the following ideas to make the room arrangement and physical environment aid the group process:

- Many Sunday-school classes use a traditional, theater-style room arrangement, with chairs in rows. Rows of chairs enable late-arrivers to slip into one of the back rows without disrupting the class.
  Peacefakers, Peacebreakers, and Peacemakers is designed to provide for an open membership, meaning that group membership may change from week to week as irregular attenders, new Sunday-school members, or visitors join the group. Other teachers prefer to arrange chairs in circles so that members can see each other face-to-face. A face-to-face arrangement facilitates group sharing, although it may hinder late-arrivers or visitors from slipping in unnoticed. The facilitator can consider these seating options and determine which one of them works best for his or her group.
- Position training equipment, such as a television monitor, so that all members can easily see it.

5. *What are some guidelines for healthy group life?*

- Announce to the group that you will begin and end on time. Begin the group even if some members are still drifting in. Conclude at the designated hour. Be dependable. If a member arrives late, continue the group process matter-of-factly and without undue attention to the tardiness.
- Ask members to agree to confidentiality—what is said in the group remains in the group. Often members will share personal stories that they don't want repeated. Urge members to refrain from mentioning group matters outside the group.

- Encourage members to focus on their own actions, failures, and responsibilities rather than dwelling on others' wrongs. Discourage members from using other peoples' names or identities, especially when members speak critically about others.

How a Session in *Peacefakers, Peacebreakers, and Peacemakers* Works

1. Each group session is designed to last 50 minutes. Time increments for each segment of the session are provided in the individual session plans in this *Peacefakers, Peacebreakers, and Peacemakers Leader Guide*.

2. A feature of *Peacefakers, Peacebreakers, and Peacemakers* is that no outside preparation is required for members. A person who attends Sunday school for the first time or who has had frequent absences would not be intimidated by this class, because it requires no study previous to the Sunday-school discussion. An individual would not be in a situation to be embarrassed because he or she had not studied a lesson. However, suggested readings, devotionals, and Scripture passages are provided for the member's enhancement should he or she decide to do optional work between sessions. A great deal of enrichment will be derived if members take time for the optional work.

3. *Peacefakers, Peacebreakers, and Peacemakers* may be used in two different ways. Members may desire to take only the first six-week study and to delve no deeper. Others may wish to also take the optional second six-week study, which will enable them to dig deeper into the biblical principles of resolving conflict. In either circumstance, helps for teaching both of the six-week studies are fully provided. All the material is designed to create a memorable experience for the group member.

4. Sessions are divided into the following segments: *Introductory Time, Group Discussion Time, Preview Further Study,* and *Closure*. Suggested time increments are fur-

nished for the various segments. A variety of group experiences encourages sharing, promotes fellowship, and breaks monotony. Leaders are encouraged to follow the Holy Spirit's leading in the group experience. Allowing members to share how God is at work in their lives in their peacemaking efforts is far more important than is a sticking rigidly to an outline.

5. Leaders are encouraged to use the video that accompanies the material. Group session plans instruct leaders on how to use the video.

How to Train Leaders

1. Churches electing to study *Peacefakers, Peacebreakers, and Peacemakers* with more than one class at a time can benefit from conducting leader training several weeks before the study begins. After leaders are enlisted, ask them to commit to a two-hour training session to equip them to lead *Peacefakers, Peacebreakers, and Peacemakers* groups.

2. Ask each leader to read the introductory material and to complete week 1 in his or her *Leader Guide* and *Member Book* before attending the training.

3. If more than eight leaders attend the training session, consider dividing the group and asking another person to lead separate training for one group while you lead the other.

4. Prepare the room for the training, obtaining a video cassette projector and screen. Prepare name tags, if necessary.

5. Sample training schedule (2 hours):

a. Introduction (20 mins.). Ask participants to introduce themselves to one another. Ask each participant to tell one struggle and one victory he or she has experienced in conflict resolution.

b. Describe the plan for *Peacefakers, Peacebreakers, and Peacemakers* in your church (20 mins.). Explain the rationale for the church's emphasis on peacemaking, the benefits to the individual church member, and the benefits of the program to the church as a corporate body. Overview the plans that are being made for church preparation, promotion, enlistment, fees, and scheduling.

c. Review the main points in "How to Lead a Group in *Peacefakers, Peacebreakers, and Peacemakers*" (p. 9). Invite questions (30 mins.).

d. Review the format of the *Member Book*. Explain that the interactive format allows members to hear classroom overview and then answer questions that relate to the material shared. Review the organization of the *Leader Guide*. Direct leaders to the "Before the Session" and "After the Session" segments that are to be used to prepare for and review after each session (30 mins.).

e. Explain the importance of offering follow-up studies after members complete *Peacefakers, Peacebreakers, and Peacemakers*. For example, if the church has not offered *The Peacemaker Seminar*, it could be used to help members reinforce what they learned in *Peacefakers, Peacebreakers, and Peacemakers* and to give them an opportunity to expose friends to these concepts. Other possibilities include *Peacemaking for Families, PeaceSowers, Guiding People Through Conflict, Conflict Coaching,* and the *Reconciler Training Course* (10 mins.).

f. Lead the group leaders in conversational prayer for the upcoming studies (10 mins.). Pray for growth in the lives of individual members and in the life of the church through *Peacefakers, Peacebreakers, and Peacemakers*.

A Life-Changing Decision

Peacefakers, Peacebreakers, and Peacemakers is written with the assumption that members have already received Jesus Christ as their Savior. However, participants may possibly realize as they study that they have never invited Christ into their lives. Be alert for this possibility. (This question will be posed to members during week 3.) Be available to answer questions for members who are thinking about accepting Christ. (See "How to Find New Life in Christ", p. 144.) If necessary arrange for them to talk to a pastor or another church leader about how to grow in Christ. Encourage both new believers and earnest seekers to continue with this study. This course is designed to help people at any stage of spiritual growth.

First Six Weeks

The Slippery Slope of Conflict

GROUP SESSION 1

Before the Session

1. Secure copies of the *Peacefakers, Peacebreakers, and Peacemakers Member Book* for your group members.
2. Obtain a copy of the third edition of *The Peacemaker* by Ken Sande for displaying to participants in class. Although reading the book is optional, the instructor's leadership will be far more credible if he or she has read the book.
3. Review the Introduction (p. 5); read the *Leader Guide* material; complete the *Member Book* for week 1 of *Peacefakers, Peacebreakers, and Peacemakers*. To be most effective as a leader, read in full the Bible passages to which your study refers, such as the full passages listed alongside the four primary causes of conflict and The Slippery Slope responses. For convenience, many Scripture references appear in full in the margin; however, use your Bible for longer references.
4. Find a quiet time and place to pray for group members by name. Pray for visitors the Lord might bring to your group this week. Ask for the wisdom you need to prepare for and lead the introductory session.
5. Read "During the Session" on page 24.
6. Plan to stay within the given times for each activity. If a worship service follows your group time, remember to close in time for members to get to the church service. Allow time for members to pick up children from the child-care area.
7. For the first session, you may want to secure enough name tags for those you expect to attend.

The Lesson
By Ken Sande
Author of *The Peacemaker*

Our Lives—a Testimony through Peace

Who are peacemakers? Peacemakers are people who breathe grace. They draw continually on the goodness and power of Jesus Christ. Then they bring His love, mercy, forgiveness, strength, and wisdom to the conflicts of daily life. God delights in breathing His grace through peacemakers and in using them to dissipate anger, improve understanding, promote justice, and encourage repentance and reconciliation.

The biblical principles this material presents have been tested in hundreds of conflicts—in everything from divorce and custody battles to workplace issues to neighborhood feuds and church splits. They really work; they are badly needed.

Conflict can damage relationships severely. Worst of all, it can destroy your Christian witness. When believers disagree bitterly or freeze each other out, they do not provide a good example of Jesus' reconciling love.

The opposite is also true. When Christians learn to be peacemakers, they can make their lives a testimony to Christ's power and love.

Your study of *Peacefakers, Peacebreakers, and Peacemakers* is designed to help you become an effective peacemaker. The principles you will learn are based solidly on God's Word and work in every type of conflict—from stopping a minor disagreement between siblings to settling multi-million-dollar lawsuits.

The Four G's of Conflict Resolution

We can summarize this biblical approach to resolving conflict in these four basic principles, which are called "The Four G's":

So whether you eat or drink or whatever you do, do it all for the glory of God (1 Cor. 10:31).

You hypocrite, first take the plank out of your own eye, and then you will see clearly to remove the speck from your brother's eye (Matt. 7:5).

Brothers, if someone is caught in a sin, you who are spiritual should restore him gently (Gal. 6:1).

First go and be reconciled to your brother; then come and offer your gift (Matt. 5:24).

• **Glorify God** (see 1 Cor. 10:31). A deep desire to bring honor to God by revealing Jesus' reconciling love and power motivates a biblical peacemaker. As we focus on God, we are freed up from impulsive, self-centered decisions that worsen conflict. As we trust in God and give Him credit for helping us to do what is right, He will be honored.

• **Get the log out of your own eye** (see Matt. 7:5). Face up to what you have contributed to a dispute before you accuse others. When we honestly admit our own faults, others often will reply in kind. This may open the way for others to discuss, negotiate, and reconcile with us.

• **Gently restore** (see Gal. 6:1). When others fail to see how they have contributed to a conflict, we can graciously show them their fault. When they do not respond appropriately, Jesus tells us to involve friends, church leaders, or other objective persons. They can help encourage us to embrace repentance and restore peace.

• **Go and be reconciled** (see Matt. 5:24). We can commit to restoring damaged relationships and negotiating just agreements. By forgiving as God forgives and by seeking equitable solutions, the door is opened to genuine peace.

These principles were developed by Peacemaker Ministries, which was established in 1982 to help Christians and their churches to respond to conflict biblically. These principles have been used throughout the United States and around the world.

The gospel is the foundational "G" that provides both the model and motivation for peacemaking! The gospel teaches that God sent His Son to save us from our sins. By His grace, we can confess our wrongs, lovingly confront others, and forgive others in the way He has forgiven us.

Among other things, this study of *Peacefakers, Peacebreakers, and Peacemakers* will explain—

• when overlooking an offense is appropriate;
• how to change attitudes and habits leading to conflict;

- when to assert your rights;
- how to confront others effectively;
- when to ask the church to intervene in a conflict;
- how to deal with unreasonable people.

This study uses real-life illustrations to show practical ways to make peace. Instead of reacting to disputes in a confused, defensive, or angry manner, we can learn to respond to conflict confidently and constructively. Great fulfillment and joy results from being a peacemaker!

A Biblical View of Conflict

God's Word explains why conflicts occur and how to deal with them. Conflict may be defined as *a difference in opinion or purpose that frustrates someone's goals or desires.* This can involve everything from spouses differing over where to go on vacation to hostile arguments, such as fights, quarrels, lawsuits, or church divisions.

Four primary causes of conflict exist:
- Misunderstandings resulting from poor communication (Josh. 22:10-34).
- Differences in values, goals, gifts, calling, priorities, expectations, interests, or opinions (Acts 15:39; 1 Cor. 12:12-31).
- Competition over limited resources, such as time or money (Gen. 13:1-12).
- Sinful attitudes and habits that lead to sinful words and actions (Jas. 4:1-2).

The Slippery Slope of Conflict

The Slippery Slope of Conflict diagram on page 4 of this book illustrates the basic ways that people respond to conflict. On the left slope of the curve are the escape responses to conflict; on the right side are the attack responses; in the center are the peacemaking responses. Just as one might slip and fall by going too far to the left or right on an ice-covered hill, a person who becomes defensive or antagonistic can make matters worse and slip into more extreme reactions. To stay on top of the Slippery Slope, ask God to help you resist the tendencies to escape or attack and to learn appropriate peacemaking responses.

Escape Responses: People tend to seek escape when they want to avoid a conflict instead of resolving it, especially in the church, where many believe that all conflict is wrong or dangerous. Escape responses include—

(1) **Denial**—Pretending the conflict doesn't exist or refusing to do what is necessary to resolve it properly (Gen. 16:1-6; 1 Sam. 2:22-25).

(2) **Flight**—Running away by leaving the house, ending a friendship, quitting a job, filing for divorce, changing churches. Sometimes temporarily withdrawing from a situation in order to calm down and pray may be best. In threatening circumstances, such as physical or sexual abuse (1 Sam. 19:9-10), flight may be necessary for a time. But running usually only postpones solving the problem (Gen. 16:6-8).

(3) **Suicide**—When people believe they've lost all hope, they may attempt to take their own lives (1 Sam. 31:4). Suicide is never the right way to deal with a conflict.

When people practice these responses, they are **"Peacefaking"**, which only prolongs a conflict.

Attack Responses: People use these when they care more about winning a conflict than about preserving a relationship. Often people view a conflict as a chance to control others, assert themselves, or take advantage of someone. These responses include—

(1) **Assault**—Overcoming an opponent by verbal attacks (including gossip and slander), physical violence, or trying to damage a person financially or professionally (Acts 6:8-15).

(2) **Litigation**—Taking someone to court. Lawsuits usually damage relationships; a Christian's witness can be damaged severely. The Bible commands Christians to

settle their differences out of court whenever possible (Matt. 5:22-26, 1 Cor. 6:1-8).

(3) **Murder**—Killing someone who opposes you (Acts 7:54-58). We also are guilty of murder when we harbor anger or hatred (1 John 3:15, Matt. 5:21-22).

When people practice these responses, they are **"Peacebreaking"**, which usually destroys relationships.

The Gospel Is the Key to Staying on Top of the Slippery Slope. A true peacemaker is guided, motivated, and empowered by the gospel—the good news that God has forgiven all our sins and made peace with us through the death and resurrection of His Son (Col. 1:19-20). Through Christ He has also enabled us to break the habit of escaping from conflict or attacking others, and He has empowered us to promote genuine justice and reconciliation by using peacemaking responses (Col. 3:12-14).

Peacemaking Responses: The Bible teaches six constructive ways to resolve conflict.

Personal peacemaking

(1) **Overlook an offense**—A deliberate decision to forgive—that is, not to talk about the offense, dwell on it, or let it grow into pent-up bitterness and anger (see Prov. 19:11).

(2) **Reconciliation**—Resolving personal or relational issues through confession, loving correction, and forgiveness (see Matt. 5:23-24).

(3) **Negotiation**—Working through material issues related to money, property, or other rights. This can be done through a cooperative bargaining process in which persons reach a settlement that satisfies each side's legitimate needs (see Phil. 2:4).

Assisted peacemaking

(1) **Mediation**—If a private agreement cannot be reached, objective, outside people can meet with parties to help them communicate and explore solutions (see

A man's wisdom gives him patience; it is to his glory to overlook an offense (Prov. 19:11).

Therefore, if you are offering your gift at the altar and there remember that your brother has something against you, leave your gift there in front of the altar. First go and be reconciled to your brother; then come and offer your gift (Matt. 5:23-24).

Each of you should look not only to your own interests, but also to the interests of others (Phil. 2:4).

24

But if he will not listen, take one or two others along, so that every matter may be established by the testimony of two or three witnesses (Matt. 18:16).

Therefore, if you have disputes about such matters, appoint as judges even men of little account in the church (1 Cor. 6:4).

If he refuses to listen even to the church, treat him as you would a pagan or a tax collector (Matt. 18:17).

Matt. 18:16). Mediators may question and counsel, but they have no authority to force a solution.

(2) **Arbitration**—When a voluntary agreement cannot be reached, you may appoint one or more arbitrators to listen to both sides and decide how to settle the issue (see 1 Cor. 6:4).

(3) **Accountability**—If a professing Christian refuses to be reconciled, Jesus commands the person's church leaders to formally intervene to hold the person accountable to Scripture and to promote repentance, justice, and forgiveness (see Matt. 18:17). This loving and restorative act can be the key to peace and restored relationships.

During the Session

Introductory time (10 mins.)

1. Welcome each person and invite each to make a name tag, if group members are not well acquainted. As members arrive, introduce each one to the others in the room if they don't already know each other. Let everyone visit informally until time to begin.

2. Distribute to each participant a *Member Book*. Direct members to their week-1 lesson guide on page 9. Explain that they will use the *Member Book* in class as they take notes (in its margins and in other spaces provided), write down personal applications, watch the accompanying video, and engage in discussions with other class members.

3. Tell members that they will begin using the *Member Book* as they participate in the following icebreaker: Working in pairs, ask each person to briefly write down (item 1, page 9) a time in which he or she was unaware about how to solve a conflict. Explain to members that this could be a dispute with a co-worker, with a family member, or in a church setting. Urge them to avoid giving specific names or identifying facts, if possible. (As leader share an example from your own life, such as this: *I*

once had a conflict with a neighbor whose children played in my flower beds and damaged my roses. I yelled at his children; this caused a breach in our relationship. I wish I had known how to handle this more peaceably.) If you answer the questions in about 45 seconds, most of the members will, also. After members have written their description of a conflict, ask each to turn to his or her partner and describe the conflict to that person. After about two minutes of sharing, ask for a volunteer to share his or her answer with the entire group.

4. Explain that this new, six-week study called *Peacefakers, Peacebreakers, and Peacemakers* is designed to provide answers to challenging questions about conflicts such as the ones the group members just discussed.

5. Hold up a copy of *The Peacemaker.* Suggest to members that they might want to purchase their own copies of this book, to which they can refer for more detailed information throughout the six-week course. For example, the Four G's of conflict resolution that you are about to share are explained more fully in *The Peacemaker.*

Group discussion (35 mins.)

6. Give a brief, three-minute overview of "Our Lives—a Testimony through Peace" and "The Four G's of Conflict Resolution" in today's lesson. As you explain the Four G's of resolving conflict, suggest that members jot down brief notes in the space provided under item 2 in the *Member Book.* After you finish the overview and members have jotted down the high points of your overview, ask each to put a star beside the "G" of conflict resolution that the person believes is most difficult for him or her to accomplish. (As leader you might share an illustration such as this: *In my own life, "Go be reconciled" is most difficult for me. I have difficulty knowing what to say to someone when I encounter the person after the conflict.)*

7. Explain that although you are group leader, you have not mastered all the concepts presented in the material but that you are a fellow struggler who wants to

become a better peacemaker. Tell members that you, like they, will share out of their own journey toward biblical peacemaking as members discuss challenges and victories.

8. Before you begin this next discussion, ask members to turn to item 3 and take a stab at writing down their definition of conflict. After giving them about 90 seconds to answer, read to the group the definition on page 21 in this guide. Then give a brief overview of the four primary causes of conflict. Ask members to write down in the *Member Book* under item 4 each of the four causes as you discuss them. Point out to members that the *Member Book* lists the biblical passages that correspond to the four causes of conflict. Tell them that space does not permit the inclusion of the full biblical text in the *Member Book*. Suggest that they look up each passage in their private study. Ask members to put a star by the cause of conflict that they believe most often fuels the conflicts they face.

9. Refer members to the Slippery Slope of Conflict diagram on page 139 in the *Member Book*. Give a brief, seven-minute review of the basic ways people respond to conflict—the escape, attack, and peacemaking responses. Direct members to item 5 in the *Member Book*. Ask them to take two minutes to complete the matching exercise based on your brief review and to indicate which responses are peacefaking ("pf"), peacebreaking ("pb"), or peacemaking ("pm"). After members have worked about two minutes on the matching exercise, tell them the answers: a,2; b,3; c,10; d,4; e,6; f,5; g,8; h,9; i,1; j,11; k,7; l,1.

(Leader: Choose between the following two activities—item 10 or 11—to use during your class-discussion time. Only in rare occasions would a leader have time to use both of these.)
10. (optional, if time allows) Show Peacemaker Parable "Gossiping about Gossip" (5 mins.). Ask members to answer questions in item 6 in the *Member Book* as they view the brief parable: Who was contributing to the conflict? *Laura, Jeff, Gina, Nancy* How? *Laura, by trying to avoid Gina and lying to her when she picked up her call on the*

answering machine. Gina, by spreading gossip. Jeff, by at first declining to get involved and then by throwing out suggestions instead of lovingly correcting Laura. Nancy, by attacking Laura (if the gossip can be believed). Which Slippery Slope responses were various people using? *Laura—denial, assault, and flight. Jeff—denial, assault, and flight. Nancy— assault. Jill—denial.* How did these people make the conflict better or worse? *None of them made the conflict better. Jeff called Laura's attention to the fact that she wasn't following biblical precepts when she wanted to "write off" Nancy, but he didn't do so in a helpful way. Only Laura, when she made the phone call to Nancy to arrange lunch, finally appeared to show some potential for healing the rift.* Which response should Laura use? *She could overlook the offense. Or, if she felt the relationship was damaged, she could go to reconcile with Nancy, as the video appeared to suggest she was trying to do.* After you show the video and give members two extra minutes to finish their questionnaires, call on volunteers to answer the questions just posed. Use the printed answers above to guide them if some hesitate to share.

11. For item 7 in the *Member Book,* instruct members to look at the "Responses to Conflict in the Bible" chart on page 12 of the *Member Book.* Ask members to indicate which Slippery Slope response to conflict was used in each situation. Mark beside each a plus sign (+) if the response was wise or a minus sign (-) if it was foolish/sinful. (In the interest of time, divide the total group into five small groups. Ask the first small group to discuss examples 1-4 and report their answers back to the class; another small group takes examples 5-8; another group, 9-12; another group, 13-16; and another group, 17-20. Or, if the time remaining is very brief, you could ask each group to report back to the large group with the answer to one of the questions answered in the small group. Later you will refer members to this chart as part of their "For Further Study" reading if they desire to look up all the recommended passages.)

Responses to Conflict in the Bible

(answers to the situations) Note: Because the Bible does not give detailed information about some of these situations, we do not know clearly whether a particular response was wise or foolish.

1. Abraham's response to the friction between Sarai-Hagar (Gen. 16:6): *Denial combined with half-hearted arbitration; foolish.*

2. Hagar's response to Sarai's persecution (Gen. 16:6-8): *Flight; foolish.*

3. Joseph's response when Potiphar's wife tried to seduce him (Gen. 39:11-12): *Flight; wise.*

4. Potiphar's wife's response when Joseph spurned her advances (Gen. 39:13-18): *Assault, apparently combined with pressing false legal charges; foolish.*

5. Pharaoh's response to the plagues God brought upon him (Ex. 7:1-12:36): *Denial; foolish.*

6. Saul's response to David when he won the hearts of the people (1 Sam.: 18:1-16): *Assault and attempted murder; foolish.*

7. David's response to Saul's attempts to kill him (1 Sam. 19:9-12): *Flight; wise (David ran away to avoid a direct confrontation with Saul).*

8. Solomon's response to the dispute over the prostitute's baby (1 Kings 3:16-28): *Arbitration or litigation (decision by the civil authority); wise.*

9. Daniel's response to the command to eat unclean food (Dan. 1:8-16): *Arbitration or litigation (decision by the civil authority); wise.*

10. Jonah's response to God's command to go to Nineveh (Jonah 1:3): *His first response was flight, which was foolish, and then he essentially acquiesced to his own death (1:12), which was tantamount to suicide; again foolish. After he repented, he listened to God (reconciliation), but then he again fell into denial and wished for death (4:1-9).*

11. Joseph's response when Herod was searching for Jesus (Matt. 2:13-15): *Flight; wise.*

12. Judas Iscariot's response to the inner conflict he felt after betraying the Lord (Matt. 27:5): *Suicide; foolish.*

13. The Corinthians' response to legal conflicts with one another (1 Cor. 6:1-8): *Litigation; foolish.*

14. The apostles' response to the conflict about distributing food (Acts 6:1-7): *Mediation and/or arbitration (their proposed solution "pleased the whole group"; we are not clear about whether it was merely a suggestion or a binding decision); wise (good leaders build consensus, not impose solutions).*

15. Barnabas' response to the conflict between Saul and the apostles (Acts 9:26-28): *Mediation; wise.*

16. Peter's response when Jewish Christians complained about teaching Gentiles (Acts 11:1-18): *Reconciliation and negotiation; wise.*

17. The Philippian slave-owners' response when Paul delivered the woman from spiritual bondage (Acts 16:16-22): *Litigation (unjust use of civil processes), resulting in assault; foolish.*

18. Paul's response to Peter's support of circumcision group (Acts 15:1-29; Gal. 2:11-21): *Reconciliation, followed by an appeal to church arbitration and accountability (counsel at Jerusalem); wise.*

19. Paul's response when charged with crimes in Jerusalem (Acts 24:1-26, 32): *Reconciliation (tried to reason with crowd), with final resort to litigation (civil authorities) after a deliberate choice to bypass church courts, which were stacked against him; wise.*

20. The Pharisees' response to Jesus: *Initially, they tried to talk ("reconcile") with Jesus. They did this not so much to understand and reason with Him but to trap Him. In the end they arrested Him and dragged Him before a corrupt church court (perverted church discipline), then took Him before a corrupt civil ruler (unjust litigation), then joined in a general assault against Him (verbal and physical), and finally instigated his murder. All that they did was foolish and sinful. Only Nicodemus responded properly to Christ (reconciliation leading to conversion).*

Bonus: God's response to our sin (the gospel): *God bears with us in our sin with great patience (Ps. 103:10-18; Rom. 9:22-24), offering and securing for us eternal forgiveness in spite of our many offenses against Him. The cost for this mercy was immeasurably great; however. God sent His Son to serve both as a mediator (1 Tim. 2:5) and as our substitute to work out a resolution to the greatest conflict the world has ever known.*

Jesus willingly went on trial in our place, was convicted for our sins (2 Cor. 5:21), and suffered the flogging, death, and separation that we deserved (Mark 15:34). The gospel is the most wonderful response to conflict that has ever occurred, but to bring it about, Jesus had to endure the most painful response to conflict that we could ever imagine.

12. Direct members to item 8 in the *Member Book*. Ask them to take two minutes to answer the question in the book, "Which of the Slippery Slope responses are you most likely to use when you are faced with a conflict? Does it usually help or hinder a resolution?" Call on a volunteer to share his or her answers with the large group.

13. Direct members to item 9 in the *Member Book*. Ask them to take two minutes to answer the question in the book, "If you were to pray for God to help you change one aspect of the way you respond to conflict, what would it be? Write that prayer below. Pray it silently as a request to God." Ask them to bow their heads and pray silently.

Preview further study (2 mins.)

14. Direct members to item 10 in the *Member Book* regarding further study. Explain to members that this study is entirely optional, but stress that they will gain far more from their study of biblical peacemaking if they take time for the extra work. Explain that the extra work for this week involves reading from *The

Peacemaker, answering all the questions on Responses to Conflict in the Bible, and reading the five daily devotionals (adapted from *The Peacemaker*). Explain that the daily devotionals provide case studies to help them see practical examples of peacemaking in action.

Closure (3 mins.)

15. As leader close in prayer. Thank God for the privilege you have of leading this *Peacefakers, Peacebreakers, and Peacemakers* group. Pray that God will give each member special insights in the following week as he or she looks for ways to practice biblical peacemaking daily. (Remind members to bring the *Member Book* next week.)

After the Session

1. Evaluate the session by listing what you believe was effective and ways you can improve.
2. Make a prayer list for each person in your group so that you can record needs to be prayed for and answers to your prayers. Pray for members. This is the best support you can give them as they seek to develop attributes of peacemakers.
3. Read "Before the Session" for group session 2 to determine the amount of preparation you will need for the next group session. At the top of the group session 2 material in this *Leader Guide,* record when you will do your preparation.
4. Carefully study week 3 and complete all the exercises in the *Member Book* so you can stay ahead of the group.

Conflict Provides Opportunities

GROUP SESSION 2

Before the Session

1. Review week 2. Read and complete the lesson for week 3 to stay ahead of the group.
2. Master this week's material in the *Leader Guide.*
3. If you are using the video or DVD, arrange for a VCR or DVD player and a monitor during the session.
4. Consider calling visitors from last week's meeting and inviting them to return. Also consider calling irregular attenders who may have been present during the week-1 session. Encourage them to return and to continue in the *Peacefakers, Peacebreakers, and Peacemakers* study.
5. Plan to stay within the given times for each activity.

The Lesson
By Ken Sande
Author of *The Peacemaker*

Not Always Bad

In last week's lesson we learned about the primary causes of conflict and the ways we can respond to it. Conflict is not necessarily bad. In fact, the Bible teaches that *some* differences are natural and beneficial if you deal with them properly. Since God created us as unique individuals, human beings naturally have different opinions, convictions, desires, perspectives, and priorities. Many of these differences are not inherently right or wrong; they simply result from God-given diversity and personal preferences (1 Cor. 12:21-31).

When we deal with disagreements properly, they can stimulate productive dialogue, encourage creativity, promote helpful change, and generally make life more interesting for us! Therefore, seek unity in your relationships without demanding uniformity (Eph. 4:1-13). Instead of demanding that others always agree with us, we can rejoice in God's diverse creation. We can work with people who simply see things differently than we do (see Rom. 15:7).

The Bible teaches that conflict is not an occasion to force our will on others but is a chance to show God's love and power in our lives. This is what Paul told the Corinthians when religious, legal, and dietary disputes threatened to divide their church (1 Cor. 10:31-11:1).

What a radical view of conflict! This passage encourages us to look at conflict as an opportunity to glorify God, to serve others, and to grow to be like Christ. Look at each of these three opportunities.

I. Glorify God

How can we bring God praise and honor in a conflict?

a. *Trust God.* Instead of relying on your own ideas and your own answers, ask God to give you direction, even if it is totally opposite to what you want to do (see Prov. 3:5). Believe that Jesus, who has saved you and wants the best for you, is using this conflict to help you grow. Follow His lead. Stop fearing what others might do to you.

b. *Obey God.* Do what He says, without compromise. This shows others that His ways are totally good, wise, and dependable (see John 15:8).

c. *Imitate God.* See what Paul told the Ephesians who struggled with conflict (Eph. 5:1-2). Mirroring Jesus in the midst of conflict is the best way to restore peace with those who oppose us (see Eph. 4:3).

Accept one another, then, just as Christ accepted you, in order to bring praise to God (Rom. 15:7).

Trust in the Lord with all your heart and lean not on your own understanding (Prov. 3:5).

This is to my Father's glory, that you bear much fruit, showing yourselves to be my disciples (John 15:8).

Be imitators of God, therefore, as dearly loved children and live a life of love, just as Christ loved us and gave himself up for us as a fragrant offering and sacrifice to God (Eph. 5:1-2).

Make every effort to keep the unity of the Spirit through the bond of peace (Eph. 4:3).

34

For it is God who works in you to will and to act according to his good purpose (Phil. 2:13).

The law of God is in his heart; his feet do not slip (Ps. 37:31).

But I tell you who love me: Love your enemies, do good to those who hate you (Luke 6:27).

Do nothing out of selfish ambition or vain conceit, but in humility consider others better than yourselves (Phil. 2:3-4).

Carry each other's burdens, and in this way you will fulfill the law of Christ (Gal. 6:2).

Brothers, if someone is caught in a sin, you who are spiritual should restore him gently (Gal. 6:1).

Always be prepared to give an answer to everyone who asks you to give the reason for the hope that you have (1 Pet. 3:15).

d. *Acknowledge God.* People will wonder how you do it when you manage conflict with grace. When they praise you, credit God for helping you do things you couldn't do on your own (see Phil. 2:13). Then go on to share the gospel with them.

Glorifying God also benefits you. Many disputes worsen when one or both sides say things hastily. Taking the four steps just mentioned makes you less inclined to stumble (see Ps. 37:31). You also will depend less on results. Even if others don't respond to your efforts, you can know the joy of obeying God.

One of the best ways to take these four steps is to ask yourself, "How can I please and honor God in this situation? How can I bring praise to Jesus and show He has saved me and is changing me?"

II. Serve Others

From a worldly perspective, seeking to serve others in the midst of conflict sounds absurd. The world says, "Look out for Number One." But Jesus says, "Love your enemies" (see Luke 6:27).

a. *Help an opponent to find better solutions to his or her problems than the person would have developed alone* (see Phil. 2:3-4). Find creative ways to satisfy both your and your opponents' needs.

b. *Carry an opponent's burdens by providing for his or her spiritual, emotional, or material needs* (see Gal. 6:2). Sometimes people lash out at you because they have other frustrations in their lives. Don't take on their problems; help them lift woes that are beyond their abilities.

c. *Help others learn where they have erred and need to change* (see Gal. 6:1). This likely involves a private conversation or may involve others in the church.

d. *Introduce others to Christ* (see 1 Pet. 3:15). Those who watch you display wisdom and self-control may wonder what the source of your power is, which may open the door for your Christian testimony.

e. *Teach and encourage others by your example* (see 1 Cor. 4:12). What your children and others learn from watching your example may impact the way they handle conflict at school, in the workplace, and in their own marriages.

III. Grow to Be Like Christ

Most conflicts offer an opportunity to grow to be Christlike. The process of conforming you to the likeness of Christ (see Rom. 8:29) began at your conversion and will continue throughout your life. Conflict may

a. *Remind you of your weaknesses and encourage you to depend more on Him* (see 2 Cor. 12:8-9). Paul's thorn in the flesh is a good example of this dependence.

b. *Expose sinful attitudes and habits in your life* (see Ps. 119:67). When pride, bitterness, and unforgiveness are exposed during conflict, you'll have the opportunity to ask God to help you overcome them.

c. *Draw on His grace to practice new attitudes and habits* (see 2 Cor. 5:17). Growth occurs when you repeatedly think and act properly when challenged.

God's process is sometimes called the "ABC of Spiritual Growth": **A**dversity **B**uilds **C**haracter. Focus more on *growing* through conflict instead of fretting about *going* through conflict.

During the Session

Introductory time (10 mins.)
1. Begin the session on time even if all members are not yet present. Begin with prayer for today's activities.
2. If visitors or members are present who did not attend last week's kickoff session, give them each a *Member Book*. Direct members to their week-2 lesson guide.
3. As an introductory activity, ask each person to write his or her personal answer to item 1 on page 18 in the *Member*

When we are cursed, we bless; when we are persecuted, we endure it; when we are slandered, we answer kindly (1 Cor. 4:12).

For those God foreknew he also predestined to be conformed to the likeness of his Son. (Rom. 8:29).

Three times I pleaded with the Lord to take it away from me. But he said to me, "My grace is sufficient for you, for my power is made perfect in weakness" (2 Cor. 12:8-9).

Before I was afflicted I went astray, but now I obey your word (Ps. 119:67).

Therefore, if anyone is in Christ, he is a new creation; the old has gone, the new has come! (2 Cor. 5:17).

Book: One way that I tried to remember to act as a Christian would during a conflict situation (preferably during the past week.) (As leader share an example from your own life, such as, *My family received the wrong order at a fast-food restaurant. A customer standing beside me also had a complaint and was yelling loudly at the clerk. I tried to remain calm and be courteous as I explained my problem. The clerk corrected my order and thanked me for not being rude.*) Ask members to pair off after writing their answers. Ask each person to share his or her answer with his or her partner. After about two minutes of sharing, ask a volunteer to share his or her answer with the group.

Group discussion (35 mins.)

4. Give a two-minute summary of the section "Not Always Bad" in today's lesson. Then ask members to answer item 2: Think of a personality or temperament difference between you and someone to whom you relate (spouse, child, co-worker, etc.). Describe how that difference can actually benefit you and the other person. (As leader you might share something like this: *My spouse is a saver; I'm a spender. Together, we act as a check-and-balance system for each other.*) After members have spent about a minute writing their answers, call on a volunteer to share his or her response with the class.

5. Give a two-minute overview of the section, "Glorify God," explaining the four ways you can bring praise and honor to Him in conflict. Ask members to write their answers to item 3 in the *Member Book*: Describe a time you responded to conflict in a way that might have appeared "unnatural" to others but which you used as an opportunity to testify to God's power. (As leader you might give an example like this: *My sister did not invite me to my niece's engagement party. At the next family outing I was kind to my sister, as though nothing had happened. Other family members who knew of the snub asked me how I could keep from being rude in return. I explained that God had helped me not to carry a grudge.*) After about two minutes have

elapsed, call on a volunteer willing to share his or her answer.

6. Give a two-minute overview of the section "Serve Others." Direct members to part II of item 3 in the *Member Book*. Instruct members, *As I describe these means of service through conflict, put a star by one way that you will commit to serving others in the days ahead.*

7. Direct members to part III of item 3 in the *Member Book*, "Grow to Be like Christ." Ask them to look up the Scripture that corresponds to the three ways people can become more Christlike through conflict. Ask them to write in the blanks the three ways, based on what they read in the Scriptures. Then give a two-minute overview based on the section "Grow to Be Like Christ."

(Leader: choose between the following two activities to use during your class discussion time. Only in rare occasions would a leader have time to use both of these.)

8. (optional, if time allows) Show the Peacemaker Parable "The Walls Come Tumbling Down" (9 mins.). Ask members to answer questions in item 4 in the *Member Book* as they view the brief parable: What Slippery Slope response was the father using? *Attack, threatening to murder Brett, then reconciliation and negotiation with Megan.* What responses was Helen using? *Attack, temporary escape when she left Bob alone.* What response was Megan using? *Escape.* How could the family turn this conflict into an opportunity to glorify God, serve other people, and grow to be like Christ? *The family could peaceably work out a solution that would be best for the future of Megan, Brett, and the baby. They could share their family's crisis with the church. This would enable church members to see a pastor's family model Christ's strength and grace in the midst of difficulty. It also would enable church members to love and support the struggling family through it.*

9. For item 5 in the *Member Book*, ask members to turn to the Recurring Themes of Peace section on page 20.

(In the interest of time, divide the total group into five small groups. Ask each group to read the verses mentioned in the section and determine what theme about peace the passages suggest. Ask each group to report back to the large group with the answer.) Answers: a. (Rom. 15:33; 2 Cor. 13:11; Phil. 4:9; Heb. 13:20; Judg. 6:24) *Peace is part of God's character, for He is frequently referred to as "the God of peace."* b. (Lev. 26:6; Num. 6:24-26; Judg. 5:31; Ps. 29:11; 119:165; Prov. 16:7; Mic. 4:1-4; Gal. 6:16) *Peace is one of the great blessings that God gives to those who follow Him.* c. (Ps. 34:14; Jer. 29:7; Rom. 14:19; 1 Cor. 7:15; 2 Cor. 13:11; Col. 3:15; 1 Thess. 5:13; Heb. 12:14) *God repeatedly commands His people to seek and pursue peace.* d. (Num. 25:12; Isa. 54:10; Ezek. 34:25; 37:26; Mal. 2:5) *God describes His covenant with His people in terms of peace.* e. (Judg. 6:23; 1 Sam. 16:5; Luke 24:36; 1 Sam. 1:17; 2 Kings 5:19; Luke 7:50; 8:48; Rom. 1:7; 15:13; Gal. 1:3; 2 Thess. 3:16) *God teaches His people to use the word peace (Hebrew, "shalom", and Greek, "eirene") as a standard form of greeting and parting.*

10. Direct members to item 6 in the *Member Book*. Ask them to think about which of the three opportunities in conflict—to glorify God, to serve others, and to grow to be like Christ—is the easiest and which one is the most difficult for them. Ask them to write a response in their book.

11. Direct members to item 7 in the *Member Book*. Ask them to take two minutes to answer the question in the book: If you were to pray for God to help you change one way in which you view conflict so you can begin seeing it as an opportunity, what would it be? Write that prayer below. Bow your heads now, and pray it silently as a request to God.

Preview further study (2 mins.)

12. Direct members to item 8 in the *Member Book* regarding further study. Remind members that this study is

optional but will help members gain more from their study of *Peacefakers, Peacebreakers, and Peacemakers*. Explain that the extra work for this week involves reading from *The Peacemaker*, finding answers to all the questions in the Recurring Theme of Peace in the Bible section (not just the answers that the member's group discovered but the answers for the entire exercise), reading the five daily devotionals (adapted from *The Peacemaker*), and completing the exercise, "If You Are Presently Involved in a Conflict."

Closure (3 mins.)
13. Call on volunteers to lead the closing prayer. Ask any member who feels led to ask God to help him or her look for ways in the week ahead to turn situations of potential conflict into times of opportunity and growth.

After the Session

1. Evaluate the session by listing what you believe was effective. Consider ways to improve in future sessions.
2. Pray daily for each group member. Record prayers prayed and prayers answered.
3. Read "Before the Session" for group session 3 to determine the amount of preparation you will need for the next group session. At the top of the group session 3 material in this *Leader Guide* record when you will do your preparation.
4. Carefully study week 4 and complete all the exercises in the *Member Book* so you can stay ahead of the group.

Conflict Starts In the Heart

GROUP SESSION 3

What causes fights and quarrels among you? Don't they come from your desires that battle within you? You want something but don't get it. You kill and covet, but you cannot have what you want. You quarrel and fight. You do not have, because you do not ask God (Jas. 4:1-3).

Someone in the crowd said to him, "Teacher, tell my brother to divide the inheritance with me." Jesus replied, "Man, who appointed me a judge or an arbiter between you?" Then he said to them, "Watch out! Be on your guard against all kinds of greed; a man's life does not consist in the abundance of his possessions." (Luke 12:13-15).

Before the Session

1. Review week 3. Read and complete the lesson for week 4 to stay ahead of the group. Master this week's material in the *Leader Guide*.
2. If you are using the video or DVD, arrange for a VCR or DVD player and a monitor during the session.
3. Contact all members of the group to ask them how they are relating to the material in *Peacefakers, Peacebreakers, and Peacemakers*. If any says he or she is completing the optional work, encourage the person in that process and offer to help with any challenges he or she may encounter.
4. Plan to stay within the given times for each activity.

The Lesson
By Ken Sande
Author of *The Peacemaker*

Unmet Desires

Our heart is the wellspring of all our thoughts, words, and actions. Therefore, it is also the source of our conflicts (see Jas. 4:1-3 and Luke 12:13-15).

These passages describe the root cause of conflict— unmet desires in our hearts. When we want something and believe we will not be satisfied unless we obtain it, that desire can start to control us. If others fail to meet our desires, we sometimes condemn them in our hearts and fight more diligently to get our own way. Here's how this progression works:

The Progression of an Idol

1. I Desire

Conflict always begins with some kind of desire. Some desires, such as vengeance, lust, or greed, are inherently wrong, but other desires are not.

Wanting such things as a loving spouse, a new computer, a growing church, or job success, is fine, if you seek them reasonably.

If someone stands in the way of a good desire, you can talk together about it and work out some agreement. But what if the other person persistently fails to satisfy your desire? You can fire the person if he or she is an employee or seek a new job if the person is your boss.

Whom have I in heaven but you? And earth has nothing I desire besides you (Ps. 73:25).

But with a family member or friend, you can't abandon relationships easily. You can trust God and seek your fulfillment in Him (see Ps. 73:25). You can continue to love the person and ask God to open doors in His good time (see Luke 6:27).

But I tell you who hear me: Love your enemies, do good to those who hate you (Luke 6:27).

Sometimes we follow another course. We fight for our desires and allow them to control us. This can destroy important relationships and draw us away from God.

2. I Demand

Next, we begin seeing unmet desires as something we deserve and therefore must have in order to be happy. We tell ourselves such things as "I work diligently all week. I deserve peace and quiet when I get home"; "I spend hours managing our budget. A new computer could save me hours of work"; "I've worked longer than anyone else on this project. I deserve the promotion."

When we see something as essential to our fulfillment, "I wish I could have this" evolves into "I must have this."

42

It becomes an idol—not an idol of wood, stone, or metal that pagans worship but anything we love and pursue more than we do God (see Luke 12:29). Even sincere Christians struggle with this.

And do not set your heart on what you will eat or drink; do not worry about it (Luke 12:29).

How can you know if a good desire may have become a sinful demand? Ask yourself these "X-ray" questions:

- What preoccupies me? What is the first thing on my mind in the morning and the last thing on my mind at night?
- What goes in this blank—"If only _____, I would be happy, fulfilled, and secure"?
- Do I want something so much that I would disappoint or hurt others in order to have it?
- When a certain desire is not met, do I feel frustration, anxiety, resentment, bitterness, depression, anger?

Such "wisdom" does not come down from heaven but is earthly, unspiritual, of the devil . . . .. Submit yourselves, then, to God. Resist the devil, and he will flee from you (Jas. 3:15, 4:7).

3. I Judge

When others fail to satisfy our desires, we criticize and condemn them in our hearts if not with our words. This causes us to imitate the devil (see Jas. 3:15; 4:7). Scripture tells us that we must evaluate others in order to respond to them in appropriate ways. This even may involve loving confrontation (see Gal. 6:1). But we cross the line when we judge others, which often is revealed by feelings of superiority, indignation, bitterness, or resentment.

Brothers, if someone is caught in a sin, you who are spiritual should restore him gently (Gal. 6:1).

The closer we are to others, the more likely we are to judge them when they fail to meet our expectations. You may say to your spouse, "If you really loved me, you, above all people, would meet my need." This may also occur with relatives, close friends, or fellow church members. Instead of giving people room to disagree or to fail, we rigidly impose our expectations on them. When they refuse to comply, our conflicts with them intensity.

4. I Punish

Whether deliberately or unconsciously, we find ways to punish people so that they give into our desires. We can lash out with hurtful words. We can pout, sulk, or look gloomy. We even can resort to physical violence or sexual abuse. We can act cool toward someone; withhold affection or physical contact; refuse to make eye contact; send subtle, unpleasant cues over a long period of time; or abandon the relationship entirely. As James 4:1-3 teaches, sinfully inflicting pain on others is a sure sign that an idol—something other than God—is ruling our hearts.

The Cure for an Idolatrous Heart

Jesus commands us to love, fear, and trust God only (see Matt. 22:37). When we long for something other than God, we deserve God's wrath and judgment.

1. Deliverance from Judgment
God provided deliverance from our idolatry by sending His Son to experience the punishment that we, as sinners, deserve. Through Jesus Christ we can become righteous in God's sight and find freedom from sin and idolatry (see Rom. 8:1-2). To receive this forgiveness and freedom, we acknowledge our sin, repent of it, and trust Jesus (see Acts 3:19). When we do, we no longer are under God's judgment. This is the good news of the gospel—forgiveness and eternal life through Jesus Christ. Each of us can claim His promise of eternal life by repenting of our sins, asking His forgiveness, and claiming Him as Savior. (See "How to Find New Life in Christ", p. 144).

2. Deliverance from Specific Idols
God not only wants to deliver us from our general problem with sin and idolatry but also from the specific, day-to-day idols that consume and control us. He calls on us to identify and confess our idols one by one. Then He calls us to follow Him as He removes them bit by bit from our hearts. He does this in three ways.

First, He uses the Bible like a spotlight to shine His Word of truth into our hearts (see Heb. 4:12). As we dili-

Jesus replied: "Love the Lord your God with all your heart and with all your soul and with all your mind" (Matt. 22:37).

Therefore, there is now no condemnation for those who are in Christ Jesus, because through Christ Jesus the law of the Sprit of life set me free from the law of sin and death (Rom. 8:1-2).

Repent, then, and turn to God, so that your sins may be wiped out, that times of refreshing may come from the Lord (Acts 3:19).

For the word of God is living and active. Sharper than any double-edged sword, it penetrates even to dividing soul and spirit, joints and marrow; it judges the thoughts and attitudes of the heart (Heb. 4:12).

For it is God who works in you to will and to act according to his good purpose (Phil. 2:13).

Brothers, if someone is caught in a sin, you who are spiritual should restore him gently (Gal. 6:1).

Delight yourself in the Lord and he will give you the desires of your heart (Ps. 37:4).

gently study it, it will reveal your idolatrous desires and show you how to love and worship God with all that you are.

Second, God uses the Holy Spirit to convict you and to help you pursue a godly life (see Phil. 2:13).

Finally, He has established the church, where spiritually mature Christian brothers and sisters can teach you, encourage you, and hold you accountable for your idols (see Gal. 6:1). In the church you can sit under godly preaching to help you better understand God's Word.

You can learn to find your greatest joy in thinking about God, meditating on His Word, talking to others about Him, praising Him, and thanking Him. As you delight more and more in Him, He will fulfill your desires with the best gift—more of Himself. You'll feel less need to find happiness, fulfillment, and security in things of this world (see Ps. 37:4).

During the Session

Introductory time (10 mins.)

1. Start the class on time. Ask for prayer requests. As leader pray for the requests named.

2. Give a *Member Book* to any person who is new to your group. Direct members to their week-3 lesson guide on page 28.

3. To introduce the session, ask each person to write his or her personal answer to item 1 in the *Member Book*: Think of one person whom you have observed dealing with conflict in a Christlike way. This conflict may have been recent or may have happened years ago. Describe what impressed you about how the person acted in the midst of the conflict. (As leader share an example from your own life, such as, *My wife refereed an argument between our two children. She asked each to name what he or she had contributed to the squabble. Then she asked each to apologize*

*specifically to the other one. This kept either one from playing
the Blame Game with each other.*) Ask whether a volunteer
would be willing to share his or her written answer with
the group. As leader stop and thank God for the example
each member wrote. Ask God to help each member exem-
plify good conflict-solving skills.

Group discussion (35 mins.)

4. Give a five-minute overview of the section "The Progression of an Idol", including descriptions of each stage
in the progression: I Desire, I Demand, I Judge, and
I Punish. Have them fill in the blanks in item 2. Ask members to answer item 3: Use these X-ray questions to identify desires that may have become idols:

- *What preoccupies me? What is the first thing on my
  mind in the morning and the last thing on my mind at
  night?*
- *What goes in this blank — "If only _____, I would
  be happy, fulfilled, and secure"?*
- *What is something I want so much that I would disappoint
  or hurt others in order to have it?*
- *When a certain desire is not met, do I feel frustration, anxiety, resentment, bitterness, anger, or depression?*

Before you ask them to get started, give an example
from your own life, such as, *I once became involved in a one-
way relationship with a friend. I believed that my world would
fall apart if I did not have this person's approval. I let my
family down by spending unnecessary time making her
casseroles and bringing her needlepoint gifts. I was consumed
with ways to make this person like me and felt depressed
because I couldn't make it work.* After about five minutes
have elapsed, call on a volunteer willing to discuss what
he or she wrote.

5. Present a two-minute overview of the section "The
Cure for an Idolatrous Heart." As you summarize the
material "Deliverance from Judgment", be sensitive to
members who never may have trusted Christ as Savior.
Direct members to page 141 in the *Member Book*, "How to

Find New Life in Christ", if they need further explanation of how to take this step. State that you will be available after class to anyone who has never taken this step of receiving forgiveness and eternal life through Jesus Christ. Then, direct members to item 4 in the *Member Book*. Ask members to look up the Scriptures that identify three ways that God provides to deliver us from specific idols. Ask them to write the way in the blank beside each Scripture. Then ask them to put a star by the one way that they will commit to using, by God's grace, in the days ahead for their deliverance.

(Leader: choose between the following two activities to use during your class-discussion time. Only in rare instances would a leader have time to use both of these.)
6. (optional, if time allows) Show Peacemaker Parable "Repentance" (6 mins.). Ask members to answer the questions in item 5 of the *Member Book* as they view the brief parable: What got things off to a bad start in the conflict? *Jack asked his wife to share some things for which she needs to repent instead of admitting his own wrongs.* What Slippery Slope responses did the couple use? *Both attacked initially, then reconciled.* What was the turning point in the conversation? *When Jack took the first step and owned his sin, admitting he was trying to be God; then his wife also was willing to admit her sins.* What desires seemed to turn into idols? *To be understood, to have the other person admit fault.*
7. Direct members to item 6 in the *Member Book*, "Steps to Replacing Idol Worship with Worship of the True God." Divide the total group into five small groups. Ask each group to read one set of verses and to determine what steps toward replacing idol worship the Scriptures suggest. Ask each group to report back to the large group with the answer.
8. Direct members to item 7 in the *Member Book*. Ask them to describe a time in which a godly person helped them see that a good desire had grown into a controlling idol and was taking first place in their lives.

9. Direct members to item 8 in the *Member Book*. Ask them to write a brief prayer in which they ask God to help them guard their hearts against desires that grow into demands and cause conflict. Then ask them to pray this silently as a request to God.

Preview further study (2 mins.)
10. Direct members to item 9 in the *Member Book* regarding further study. Explain that this optional extra work this week involves reading from *The Peacemaker*, finding answers to the questions in "Steps in Replacing Idol Worship with Worship of the True God" (not just the answers that the member's group discovered but for the entire exercise), reading the daily devotionals (adapted from *The Peacemaker*), and completing "If You Are Presently Involved in a Conflict."

Closure (3 mins.)
11. Call for two volunteers to dismiss the group in prayer. Suggest that the members thank God that He provided deliverance from idols and that He can help us break free from desires that fuel our conflicts.

After the Session

1. Continue to evaluate your leadership. Ask God to show you ways you need to be more sensitive to members' needs during group sessions.
2. Call or meet with members whom you detect may be struggling with some of the concepts in *Peacefakers, Peacebreakers, and Peacemakers*. Encourage these members.
3. Pray daily for each group member. Remember prayer requests that members mentioned early in session 3.
4. Read "Before the Session" for group session 4 to determine the amount of preparation you will need for the next group session. At the top of the group session 4 material in this *Leader Guide* record when you will do your preparation.

Confession Brings Freedom

GROUP SESSION 4

Before the Session

1. Review week 4. Read and complete the lesson for week 5 to stay ahead of the group.
2. Master this week's material in the *Leader Guide*.
3. If you are using the video or DVD, arrange for a VCR or DVD player and a monitor during the session.
4. Pray for group members. Contact any who voiced a special prayer request last week. Express your personal concern. Assure those you call that you are praying for them.
5. Make five slips of paper to hand to small groups you will form. Write on these phrases (one phrase per slip): Controlling Others (2 Tim. 2:25), Breaking Your Word (Ps. 15:4), Failing to Respect Authority (Rom. 13:1-7), Forgetting the Golden Rule (Matt. 7:12), and Serving Sinful Desires (1 John 2:15-17).
6. Plan to stay within the given times for each activity.

The Lesson
By Ken Sande
Author of *The Peacemaker*

More than a Feeling

Repentance is the first step in gaining freedom from sin and conflict. Repentance is not something we can do on our own; God convicts us of sin and shows us the road to freedom (see 2 Tim. 2:25). Repentance involves more than a mere apology. To repent is to wake up to the fact that our ideas, attitudes, values, and goals are wrong. It involves "coming to your senses" (see Luke 15:17), leading you to renounce sin and turn to God (see Isa. 55:7).

Simply feeling bad about your sin doesn't prove you are repentant. See how Paul explains this to the Corinthians (see 2 Cor. 7:10). "Worldly sorrow" means feeling sad because you got caught and because you must suffer the consequences. Worldly sorrow often is short-lived; you may behave the same way again. In contrast "godly sorrow" means feeling bad because you have offended God. It involves a change of heart (2 Chron. 6:37-39) and changed behavior—the evidence of true repentance.

Examine Yourself

We show we are repentant when we examine ourselves in order to uncover our sins. To sin literally means "to miss the mark"—to fail to heed God's law (see 1 John 3:4). We sin against God by doing what His law forbids. We also sin against God by not doing what He requires (see Jas. 4:17). Even seemingly small wrongs against others are serious in God's eyes; every wrong violates His will (Num. 5:6-7). Failing to bear someone's burden or to gently restore him or her, for example, is a sin against God.

We don't like to admit that we have sinned. We may minimize our role by saying we simply made a mistake or erred in judgment. We blame others and avoid our contribution to the conflict. We divert attention from ourselves and avoid repentance. We eventually pay an unpleasant price, as King David discovered, when we refuse to own our sins (Ps. 32:3-5).

If you have trouble identifying and confessing your wrongs, ask God to help you see your sin clearly (Ps. 139:23-24); then ask a spiritually mature friend to counsel and correct you (see Prov. 12:15).

Those who oppose him he must gently instruct, in the hope that God will grant them repentance leading them to a knowledge of the truth (2 Tim. 2:25).

When he came to his senses, he said, "How many of my father's hired men have food to spare, and here I am starving to death!" (Luke 15:17).

Let the wicked forsake his way and the evil man his thoughts (Isa. 55:7).

Godly sorrow brings repentance that leads to salvation and leaves no regret, but worldly sorrow brings death. (2 Cor. 7:10.).

Everyone who sins breaks the law; in fact, sin is lawlessness (1 John 3:4).

Anyone, then, who knows the good he ought to do and doesn't do it, sins (Jas. 4:17).

The way of a fool seems right to him, but a wise man listens to advice (Prov. 12:15).

50

Ways We Sin

Reckless words pierce like a sword, but the tongue of the wise brings healing (Prov. 12:18).

Don't grumble against each other, brothers, or you will be judged (Jas. 5:9).

Do not testify against your neighbor without cause, or use your lips to deceive (Prov. 24:28).

A perverse man stirs up dissension, and a gossip separates close friends (Prov. 16:28).

Do not go about spreading slander among your people (Lev. 19:16).

Do not let any unwholesome talk come out of your mouths, but only what is helpful for building others up according to their needs, that it may benefit those who listen (Eph. 4:29).

We often contribute to a conflict by sinning in the following ways:

1. Using Your Tongue as a Weapon—sinful speech can take these forms:

    a. Reckless words (see Prov. 12:18)—saying what springs to mind without thinking about the consequences

    b. Grumbling and complaining (see Jas. 5:9)—which makes others feel we are critical or ungrateful

    c. Falsehood (see Prov. 24:28)—includes lying, exaggeration, telling half-truths, distorting the truth

    d. Gossip (see Prov. 16:28)—betraying a confidence or discussing unfavorable facts about others with a person who is not part of the problem or of the solution

    e. Slander (see Lev. 19:16)—speaking false and malicious words about another person

    f. Worthless talk (Eph. 4:29)—careless, critical, meaningless words not designed to benefit others

2. Controlling Others—trying to persuade, manipulate, or force others to do things that simply make us more comfortable and are convenient. Although we may genuinely care about others' decisions and offer sincere advice when asked, we overstep our boundaries when we disrespect their own decisions and persist in trying to change their minds (see 2 Tim. 2:25, p. 49).

3. Breaking Our Word—God expects us to keep our commitments, even if we make them unwisely (Eccl. 5:4-7, Ps. 15:4). If unforeseen circumstances make keeping your word difficult, you may seek release from your obligation. Sometimes you may be freed if the other party fails substantially to keep his or her word. If you cannot be released biblically, ask God to help you keep your word and learn from your mistake.

4. Failing to Respect Authority—abuse of or rebellion against the authority God has established in the church, the government, the family, and the workplace. God establishes authority to maintain peace and order (Rom. 13:1-7). He calls us to respect the *positions* of those in authority even when their *personalities* are lacking (see Matt. 23:1-3). We may appeal, perhaps offering alternatives, when a person in authority commands us to sin. If we can't persuade him or her to change, obey any instructions that do not violate Scripture and trust God to take care of the results (1 Pet. 2:19-23).

5. Forgetting the Golden Rule—which Jesus taught (see Matt. 7:12). Ask yourself questions such as, "Would I want someone else to treat me the way I have been treating _____?" or "If I owned this business, would I want my employees to behave the way I am behaving?"

6. Serving Sinful Desires—idols of the heart such as improper desires for physical pleasure, praise, and the desire to always be right (making us defensive); love of money or other material possessions (leading to envy); excessive concern about what others think about us; and good things that we want too much (a longing for love, respect, comfort, convenience, success, or achievement) (1 John 2:15-17).

The Seven A's of Confession

One way to humbly and thoroughly admit your wrongs is to use the Seven A's:

1. Address everyone involved—Confess your sin first to God and then to everyone your wrongdoings have affected. "Heart sins"—those occurring only in your thoughts and not affecting others—need only be confessed to God. But "social sins"–those felt or witnessed by others—need to be confessed to all whom they have affected (see Luke 19:8).

2. Avoid "if", "but", and "maybe"—Don't ruin or dilute a confession by minimizing your guilt. Avoid saying, "*If* I have done something to upset you, I'm sorry." "I shouldn't have lost my temper, *but* I was tired." "*Maybe* I could have tried more diligently."

The teachers of the law and the Pharisees sit in Moses' seat. So you must obey them and do everything they tell you. But do not do what they do, for they do not practice what they preach (Matt. 23:1-3).

So in everything, do to others what you would have them do to you, for this sums up the Law and the Prophets (Matt. 7:12).

But Zacchaeus stood up and said to the Lord, "Look, Lord. Here and now I give half of my possessions to the poor, and if I have cheated anybody out of anything, I will pay back four times the amount" (Luke 19:8).

I am no longer worthy to be called your son: make me like one of your hired men (Luke 15:19).

Being confident in this, that he who began a good work in you will carry it on to completion until the day of Christ Jesus (Phil. 1:6).

You were taught, with regard to your former way of life, to put off your old self, which is being corrupted by its deceitful desires; to be made new in the attitude of our minds; and to put on the new self, created to be like God in true right-eousness and holiness (Eph. 4:22-24).

3. Admit specifically—Specific admissions of sinful desires and actions help convince others that you are honestly facing up to what you have done. This makes forgiving you easier.

4. Acknowledge the hurt—Show that you understand how your action harmed the person, such as in the following example: "You must have been embarrassed when I said those things in front of everyone."

5. Accept the consequences—as the prodigal son demonstrated (see Luke 15:19). For example, you could say, "You have every right to fire me because of what I have done." When you accept consequences and work to repair any damage you have caused, the other person will find forgiving you to be easier.

6. Alter your behavior—Describe some of the attitude, character, and behavior changes you hope to make, with God's help. This indicates you take the matter seriously.

7. Ask forgiveness; allow time—Avoid pressuring; some people need time. You may need to say, "I hope you will soon be able to forgive me, because I want very much to be reconciled. Meanwhile, I will do my best to repair the damage. If I can do more, please let me know."

A fairly simple statement of confession suffices for minor offenses. The more serious the offense, the wiser to work through all Seven A's. Ask God to help you avoid turning this process into a meaningless ritual. Remember that you are serving the person you offended and not merely gaining comfort for yourself. Be prepared to fulfill your commitment regardless of the person's response.

You Can Change

God desires to help us grow and change (see Phil. 1:6). He gave us a new mind and a new nature when we trusted Jesus (see Eph. 4:22-24). He can help us replace sinful behavior with godly attitudes and habits. To change, we can (1) pray—Ask Him for faith to believe you can change and for help in replacing old ways with new ways; (2) delight yourself in the Lord—Focusing on Him shows us that He can provide what idols promise but can't deliver; (3) study—Regular study of His Word helps us understand His ways so that our minds are "made new"; and (4) practice—Carefully monitor yourself to control your tongue in an argument. Ask God to help you forgive when someone offends. Faithful practice can help you flex your repentance muscles so you truly can become a peacemaker.

During the Session

Introductory time (10 mins.)

1. Greet members as they arrive. Begin on time. Ask for a brief report on answered prayer; take new prayer requests. Open the session with prayer, or call on a volunteer to do so.

2. Hand out a *Member Book* to anyone who may have just joined your group. Direct members to their week-4 lesson guide on page 39.

3. As an introductory activity, ask each person to write his or her personal answer to item 1 in the *Member Book*: Think back on a conflict you have had with another person. Describe one way you contributed to that conflict. (As leader share an example from your own life, such as, *My daughter consistently refused to clean up her room. This resulted in a huge disagreement between us. I realized that my constant goading at her was causing her to rebel. I apologized for nagging her. We developed new policy guidelines with logical consequences, such as loss of phone privileges, when her room was in disarray. This worked much more peaceably than did my constant intervention.*) Ask members to pair off after writing their answers. Ask each person to share his or her answer with the fellow group member. (Make sure group members are sharing with different persons and not the same individual week after week.) After about two min-

utes of sharing, ask for a volunteer willing to share his or her answer to the question with the rest of the group.

Group discussion (35 mins.)

4. Give a brief, two-minute (total) summary of the sections, "More than a Feeling" and "Examine Yourself." Make certain to show the difference between a quick apology and true repentance and between worldly sorrow and godly sorrow. Explain the harm of minimizing our role in a conflict. Then ask members to answer item 2 in the *Member Book*: After reading the following case studies, put a check beside the one that demonstrates true repentance. After members have spent about 90 seconds on this exercise, call for a volunteer to share his or her answer. *(The correct answer is c: the discussion between Angela and April. Mary's apology is conditional, since she states what she thinks Todd did wrong as well. Michael expresses worldly sorrow but not godly sorrow for what he has done.)*

5. Direct members to number 1 under item 3, "Using Our Tongue as a Weapon", in the *Member Book*. Ask members to complete the matching exercise. (Answers: *a,6; b,1; c,5; d,4; e,2; f,3)* Ask members as a group to call out the correct answers as you read the type of damage in the first column. Then, if time permits, call for a volunteer to read some of the Scriptures that correspond to the type of damage.

6. Ask members to form five groups. State that in the previous exercise they learned about one of the ways we sin (using our tongues as a weapon) that contributes to conflict. Tell the small groups that you will ask them to each summarize one of the remaining ways that we sin (numbers 2-6 under item 3). Give each group one of the pieces of paper you made before class, which lists one of the remaining ways we sin and a supporting Scripture. Ask groups to take about five minutes discussing what they think the sin involves and how we sin when we perform this act. Ask them to give a one-minute report to the class.

During the reports, ask members to jot down in the *Member Book* under the correct five categories a time that they remember sinning in this manner. After each group reports, you as leader may add insights from the *Leader Guide.*

7. Give a five-minute summary of the Seven A's of Confession. As you summarize, direct members to the Seven A's of Confession list on page 41 of the *Member Book.* Under item 4 in the *Member Book,* ask members to put a star by the "A" of confession that they consider the most difficult for them.

8. Give a one-minute summary of the section, "You Can Change." Ask each member to write a brief prayer to God, asking for help with the "A" in the Seven A's of Confession that he or she starred in item 4.

(Leader: Choose between the following two activities to use during your class discussion time. Only in rare occasions would a leader have time to use both of these.)

9. Show Peacemaker Parable "I'm Really Sorry" (4 mins.). Ask members to answer questions in item 6 of the *Member Book* as they view the brief parable: What was wrong with the husband's apology? *It was nonspecific, he resorted to namecalling, and it appeared insincere because it was done for his own convenience so he could go to watch the game.* How did the wife contribute to the conflict? *She sulked and made her husband play a guessing game about what had offended her. She could have helped by using an "I-feel" message, such as, "I felt hurt when you made the comments about women in the workforce." This would have clarified matters.*

10. Direct members to item 7, "A Fast Turnaround", in the *Member Book.* Ask them to read the story and answer the questions pertaining to it below the story.

11. Direct members back to item 5 in the *Member Book.* Ask them to bow their heads and silently pray to God the prayer they wrote there.

Preview further study (2 mins.)

12. Direct members to item 8 in the *Member Book* regarding further study. Explain that the extra work this week involves reading from *The Peacemaker*, reading and finding answers to "A Fast Turnaround", reading the five daily devotionals (adapted from *The Peacemaker*), and completing "If You Are Presently Involved in a Conflict." Ask whether members at this point have any questions regarding their further study.

Closure (3 mins.)

13. Ask members to pair off. Give them these instructions: "Share with your partner one area regarding this week's study that you believe is most challenging for you. For example, you may believe that avoiding gossip and slander is most difficult, or you may find that accepting the consequences for your actions is very challenging." Ask members to conclude by praying for each other about the issues raised during this sharing time.

After the Session

1. Make a list of areas in which you believe you demonstrated leadership during the session. Then jot down ways you will strive to improve during next week's session.
2. Pray about the events that transpired during the session just concluded. Thank God for His activity in the midst of the session. Ask the Holy Spirit to continue to stir each member's heart during the week ahead, so each can practically apply lessons learned.
3. Read "Before the Session" for group session 5 to determine the amount of preparation you will need for the next group session. At the top of the group session 5 material in this *Leader Guide* write when you will do your preparation.

Just Between the Two of You

GROUP SESSION 5

Before the Session

1. Review week 4. Read and complete the lesson for week 5 to stay ahead of the group.
2. Master this week's material in the *Leader Guide*.
3. If you are using the video or DVD, arrange for a VCR or DVD player and a monitor during the session.
4. Pray daily for each group member. Ask the Lord to give you the wisdom you need to prepare for the group session.
5. Plan to stay within the given times for each activity. However, remember that allowing members to share freely is more important than is sticking to a plan you develop for the group session. By this point in the series, group members may be arriving at a session eager to share about something that happened in their lives related to the material studied. Be sensitive to the Holy Spirit's work in your group.

The Lesson
By Ken Sande
Author of *The Peacemaker*

Opportunities to Serve

Although simply overlooking another person's sins often is best, times arise when doing so only prolongs alienation and encourages the person to continue acting hurtfully.

One of the most challenging ways to serve another person in the midst of conflict is to help that person see where he or she has been wrong and needs to change. Here are some basic guidelines on when and how you can go and talk privately with another person about his or her contribution to the conflict.

Restoring Means More than Confronting

If your brother sins against you, go and show him his fault, just between the two of you. If he listens to you, you have won your brother over (Matt. 18:15).

Do not rebuke an older man harshly, but exhort him as if he were your father. Treat younger men as brothers (1 Tim. 5:1).

Do everything without complaining or arguing (Phil. 2:14).

Jesus calls for something beyond simply confronting others with a list of their wrongs. Focusing on Matthew 18:15, we think we must always confront directly to force others to admit they've sinned. However, note the second part of the verse: "If he listens to you, you have won your brother over." This clearly implies that Jesus had restoration in mind. As does the context of the rest of chapter 18, Matthew 18:12-14 speaks of a loving shepherd seeking a wandering sheep and rejoicing when it is found. In verses 21-35, the parable of the unmerciful servant reminds us to be merciful and forgiving, just as God is to us.

Although direct confrontation sometimes is necessary, the Scriptures clearly show other valid ways exist to confront people about their wrongs. The Bible calls us to use confessing, teaching, instruction, reasoning with, showing, encouraging, correcting, warning, admonishing, or rebuking—depending on the person's position and the urgency of the situation (see 1 Tim. 5:1). The Bible also warns us not to degenerate into quarreling, arguing, or foolish controversies (see Phil. 2:14).

Jesus used questions and discussion that caused the Samaritan woman to assess her own life (John 4:1-18). His parables and stories helped other people see their sins (Matt. 21:33-45; Luke 15). Paul engaged the Athenians in a point of common interest instead of hitting them head on with their idolatry (Acts 17:22-31). Esther took two days and two banquets to show the king the wrong of decreeing that all Jews should be killed (Esther 5-7). In the same way God can work in us to discern the way, time, and place to approach someone.

Sooner or Later, Face-to-Face

Immediate, face-to-face meetings can be an important step to reconciliation, but this is not the only way to begin the process. Sometimes you first may involve others to act as neutral intermediaries.

Jacob sent servants and gifts ahead to set the stage for a friendly encounter with his brother, Esau (Gen. 32-33). Joseph's brothers sent someone to speak on behalf of them to appeal for mercy (see Gen. 50:15-17). Abigail intervened between her husband and an enraged David (1 Sam. 2:18-35). Barnabas spoke to the apostles on the newly converted Saul's behalf (see Acts 9:26-27).

Here are some occasions when involving other people may work best:
- When you deal with a person from a culture or tradition in which resolving problems through intermediaries is customary
- When going to someone privately will make him or her lose face in others' sight
- When either party might feel intimidated by the other person, perhaps because verbal skills or positions of authority or influence are different
- When one person was abused by the other and a possibility exists that the abuser will use a private conversation to manipulate or silence the abused person
- When a third party, closer to the person who may be caught in sin, is willing to raise the issue with the offender

Regardless of how the process begins, the Bible teaches that a face-to-face meeting usually is essential at some point. Scripture tells of several marvelous reconciliations that occurred after personal meetings: Jacob and Esau (Gen. 33:6-12); Joseph and his brothers (Gen. 45:1-5); and

When Joseph's brothers saw that their father was dead, they said, "What if Joseph holds a grudge against us and pays us back for all the wrongs we did to him?" So they sent word to Joseph, saying, "Your father left these instructions before he died. 'This is what you are to say to Joseph: I ask you to forgive your brothers the sins and the wrongs they committed in treating you so badly'" (Gen. 50:15-17).

When he came to Jerusalem, he tried to join the disciples, but they were all afraid of him, not believing that he really was a disciple. But Barnabas took him and brought him to the apostles. He told them how Saul on his journey had seen the Lord and that the Lord had spoken to him, and how in Damascus he had preached fearlessly in the name of Jesus (Acts 9:26-27).

60

But the king said, "He must go to his own house; he must not see my face" (2 Sam. 14:24).

Therefore, if you are offering your gift at the altar and there remember that your brother has something against you, leave your gift there in front of the altar. First go and be reconciled to your brother; then come and offer your gift (Matt. 5:23-24).

I tell you that anyone who is angry with his brother will be subject to judgment. Again, anyone who says to his brother, 'Raca', is answering to the Sanhedrin. But anyone who says, "You fool!" will be in danger of the fire of hell (Matt. 5:22).

If your brother sins, rebuke him, and if he repents, forgive him (Luke 17:3).

Paul and the apostles (Acts 9:27-28). The story of David and Absalom is a tragic example of what can happen if offended people fail to meet face-to-face. After Absalom was pardoned and was allowed to return to Jerusalem, David refused to see him (see 2 Sam. 14:24). Joab, the intermediary, failed to urge the king to see his son. This prolonged estrangement embittered Absalom toward his father (14:28-32) and led to a rebellion in which Absalom was killed (2 Sam. 15-18).

If Someone Has Something Against You

If you learn that someone has something against you, God expects you to take the iniative to seek peace—even if you believe that the other person is totally at fault. Jesus' teaching (see Matt. 5:23-24) confirms this: you are responsible for seeking reconciliation, even if you think that person's complaints are unfounded.

You can initiate reconciliation for several other reasons: your Christian witness is at stake, you will gain a clear conscience, and you can bless your brother/sister (see Jesus' warning in Matt. 5:22 against unresolved anger). If you do not go, bitter feelings may eat away at that person and separate him or her from God.

You cannot force someone to change his or her mind about you, but you can make every effort to "live at peace" by clearing up misunderstandings and difficulties (Rom. 12:18).

When Someone's Sins Are Too Serious to Overlook

Deciding whether another person's sin is so serious that you need to go and talk to him or her is difficult. Jesus clearly teaches that this kind of attention is sometimes necessary (see Luke 17:3).

Ask yourself these questions:

1. Is it dishonoring God?—When someone's sin becomes visible enough to significantly and obviously affect his or her Christian witness, address it (see Matt. 21:12-13).

2. Is it damaging your relationship?—If your feelings, thoughts, words, or actions toward another have been altered for more than a short period of time, the offense is probably too serious to overlook.

3. Is it hurting others?—This may occur in a direct way (such as child abuse or drunken driving); it may set a bad example that might lead others astray; or it may alter the unity of the church.

4. Is it hurting the offender?—This sin may be damaging the offender (for example, alcohol abuse) or impairing his or her relationship with God or other people. Intervene when you see a brother or sister ensnared in serious sin (see Jas. 5:19-20).

If a sin does not appear to be seriously harming a brother or sister or damaging his or her relationships, simply asking God to show the person the need to change may be best. But if the sin appears to be dragging your friend under, do not delay in going to him or her.

Special Considerations

1. Going to non-Christians—The Bible commands us to do all we can to "live at peace with everyone" (Rom. 12:18). We are to be concerned with the well-being of others regardless of whether they are believers. God may use our faithful peacemaking efforts to help other people believe in Christ.

2. Going to a person in authority—Everyone sins and needs correction (see 1 Tim. 5:19-20), even a boss or church elder. Choose your words carefully and speak respectfully, affirming your regard for authority.

3. Going to an abuser—Rarely is it wise for an abused person to talk privately with his or her abuser. Consider involving others in the confrontation process. The church is responsible for helping the abuser admit the sin, accept its consequences, and get appropriate help while at the

Jesus entered the temple area and drove out all who were buying and selling there. He overturned the tables of the money changers and the benches of those selling doves (Matt. 21:12-13).

My brothers, if one of you should wander from the truth and someone should bring him back, remember this: Whoever turns a sinner from the error of his way will save him from death and cover over a multitude of sins (Jas. 5:19-20).

Do not entertain an accusation against an elder unless it is brought by two or three witnesses. Those who sin are to be rebuked publicly, so that the others may take warning (1 Tim. 5:19-20).

same time ministering lovingly and diligently to the victim.

4. Going tentatively and repeatedly—Keeping a cautious, fair-minded manner will encourage better results; remember that you may have misunderstood. Give the other person time to process the conversation; go again if your first meeting is not successful. If you decide further personal conversations are truly pointless or harmful, you may decide that overlooking the matter is wise.

After the Log Is Out of Your Eye

Why do you look at the speck of sawdust in your brother's eye and pay no attention to the plank in your own eye? How can you say to your brother, "Let me take the speck out of your eye," when all the time there is a plank in your own eye? You hypocrite, first take the plank out of your own eye, and then you will see clearly to remove the speck from your brother's eye (Matt. 7:3-5).

Jesus teaches that you are to avoid talking with someone until you deal with your contribution to the problem (see Matt. 7:3-5). Sometimes your confession prompts another to also admit his or her sin. When this doesn't occur, you may feel awkward. Bringing up the other person's wrongs may cause him or her to think your confession wasn't sincere. But if you leave without discussing the other person's contribution, the person may see no need to change. At this point you may decide to overlook the offense. Build on the other person's surface confession by saying, "I appreciate your admitting that you lost your temper, Bob. May I explain how I felt when that happened?" You may need to postpone confrontation until another time. You may choose this third step in hope that during that interval of time, the other person's behavior may change, the person may be willing to admit wrong behavior, or he or she may be moved by your efforts to deal with your faults and thus more willing to talk about it later.

With God's grace and the right words (including your own confession), such a conversation often leads to restored peace and stronger relationships.

During the Session

Introductory time (10 mins.)

1. Greet members. Ask each to think of one change in his or her life that has occurred since beginning the *Peacefakers, Peacebreakers, and Peacemakers* study. Call on three volunteers to voice sentence-long prayers thanking God for the change that he or she has just recalled.

2. Hand out a *Member Book* to anyone who may have just joined the group. Direct members to their week-5 lesson guide on page 52.

3. For this week's get-started activity, ask members to turn to item 1 of the *Member Book* and describe a time when they overlooked an offense. Then ask each to describe, where indicated, a time in which he or she decided to approach someone about a wrong that person committed. Ask members to turn to a partner and to share about both instances. (As leader you might share something like this: *A friend promised me she would take me to lunch for my birthday. I looked forward to this. When my birthday arrived, she never called to fulfill on her invitation. I felt hurt about this, but I knew that her mother had been ill and that she might have been preoccupied, so I decided to overlook this offense rather than add to her stress by confronting her.* Regarding the time you chose to confront another, you might say, *At work I learned that an employer had told all the other assistant managers except me that he was contemplating a move. The contemplated new job would affect my area more directly than it would any of the other workers that he told. I approached him and, using 'I' messages, shared with him that I felt hurt and overlooked by his actions. He responded well, acknowledged his unintended slight, and apologized. Our relationship improved after the confrontation.*)

Group discussion (35 mins.)

4. Give a brief, two-minute (total) summary of the section "Opportunities to Serve" and the first two paragraphs of

"Restoring Means More than Confronting." Direct members to item 2 in the *Member Book*. Ask them to look up the verses to determine how each person—Jesus, Paul, and Esther—used alternate means to direct confrontation to point out wrongdoing to others. (Answers: *Jesus used questions and discussion to engage the Samaritan woman; he used parables and stories as round-about ways to help people see their sins; Paul engaged the Athenians on a point of common interest and moved gradually into the good news of the one true God; Esther took two days and two banquets to get to the point of telling the king about the injustice of his decree to kill all the Jews.*) Give members two minutes to write down their answers; then call on volunteers to call out the answers to the questions.

5. Give a brief, two-minute summary of the first three paragraphs of the section "Sooner or Later, Face-to-Face." Ask members to write down under item 3 in the *Member Book* the answer to the question: Have you ever used an intermediary to prepare the way before you approached someone about a problem? (Consider sharing from your own experience something like this: *I asked my choir director to approach a fellow committee member who was threatening to quit the choir because I was given a solo in the Christmas cantata instead of her. When he spoke with her, he assigned her a solo in the Easter cantata and in the process explained his rationale for assigning the Christmas soloists. This approach made her more willing to talk with me about why I felt she had been avoiding me and slandering me.*) Give members one minute to write down their answers. Call on a volunteer to share. Conclude by summarizing the remaining two paragraphs of the section, "Sooner or Later, Face-to-Face", pointing to times in which the Bible depicts the importance of face-to-face meetings, and the example of when David and Absalom failed to reconcile because no such meeting took place.

6. Involve the group in a three-minute discussion about the principles in the section, "If Someone Has Something Against You." Start by asking members such questions as,

"What do you think you should do when you feel no responsibility whatsoever for the conflict? Should you approach someone if you believe you have done nothing and that person is totally in the wrong? Would anyone be willing to share about a time in which you have done this?" Hit some of the highlights of the section "If Someone Has Something Against You", that might not have been mentioned already. Then direct members to item 4 in the *Member Book*. Ask them to answer the question of whether approaching another person who has something against them, even if they believe they did nothing to contribute to the alienation, is difficult for them.

7. Give a brief overview of the section "When Someone's Sins Are Too Serious to Overlook." Direct members to item 5 in the Member Book. Ask them to fill in the blanks of the question, "What are the four criteria for determining whether another person's sin is so serious that talking with the person is advisable?", based on your overview.

8. Direct members to item 6 in the *Member Book*. Item 6 deals with some of the matters discussed in the section "Special Considerations." Ask them to work in pairs and spend about two minutes answering these questions: How might you approach a non-Christian? How might you approach a person in authority over you? How might you approach an abuser? How might you deal with someone who has not responded well to your first approach? Ask them to write their answers in the *Member Book* as they discuss these questions. Then call for a class discussion on these matters. As leader add any important principles the discussion has not generated.

9. Direct members to item 7 in the *Member Book*. Tell them the item lists several unique situations that might occur if one of them approached someone who was guilty of wrongdoing toward him or her and apologized for his or her (the member's) part of the wrong. Ask members to write what they would do in the situations listed. As volunteers call out their answers in a group discussion,

expound on the principles found in "After the Log Is Out of Your Eye."

10. (optional, if time allows) Show Peacemaker Parable "Slippery Slope Denial" (4 mins.). Ask members to answer questions in item 8 of the *Member Book* as they view the brief parable: What aspect of the Slippery Slope was Clare following? *She was in serious denial.* What role did her daughter play? *Her daughter confronted Clare with Clare's need to approach Janet. She showed Mom that she was being harmed emotionally and spiritually by letting things fester.*

11. Ask members to say a brief, silent prayer, asking God to show them any situation in their lives in which they might need to carefully approach another person about his or her sins.

Preview further study (2 mins.)
12. Direct members to item 9 in the *Member Book* regarding further study. Explain that the extra work this week involves reading from *The Peacemaker*, reading the five daily devotionals (adapted from *The Peacemaker*), and completing "If You Are Presently Involved in a Conflict." Ask whether members have any questions regarding their further study at this point.

Closure (3 mins.)
13. Explain to members that next week, week 6, is the last week of the part-1 study of *Peacefakers, Peacebreakers, and Peacemakers*. Tell members that the group will decide next week whether to continue in the study or to move onto another topic after the week-6 lesson. Explain that the group will have another opportunity in the future to study part 2 if members do not choose to go immediately into this subsequent, six-week unit. Assure members that they will have attained much new, valuable information during this six weeks of study, regardless of whether they decide to press on in the subject.

14. As leader close in prayer. Ask God to help members as they decide whether to continue with the part-2 study.

Thank Him for each member who has participated. Ask Him to bless each during the week ahead as he or she discerns His will for confronting in conflict.

After the Session

1. Call any member you believe may need special encouragement regarding a conflict situation in his or her life. Offer to pray with the person as he or she considers whether to approach someone to reconcile a relationship.
2. Pray for members as they prepare for your final group session together. Ask that God's will be done regarding the decision to study the second part of *Peacefakers, Peacebreakers, and Peacemakers.*
3. Read "Before the Session" for group session 6 to determine the amount of preparation you will need for the next group session. At the top of the group session 6 material in this *Leader Guide* record when you will do your preparation.

Forgive As God Forgave You

GROUP SESSION 6

Before the Session

1. Review week 6. Read and complete the lesson for week 1 (part 2). Scan the material for weeks 2 through 6 so you can give a brief overview of the part-2 study.
2. Master this week's material in the *Leader Guide*.
3. If you are using the video or DVD, arrange for a VCR or DVD player and a monitor during the session.
4. Consider calling members to see if they have any questions about the material covered as well as any questions or concerns about continuing in a study of the second part of *Peacefakers, Peacebreakers, and Peacemakers*
5. Plan to stay within the given times for each activity.

The Lesson
By Ken Sande
Author of *The Peacemaker*

A High Standard

Christians are the most forgiven people in the world. Therefore, we should be the most forgiving people in the world. We know, however, that forgiving others genuinely and completely is difficult.

Forgive us our debts, as we also have forgiven our debtors (Matt. 6:12).

Too often we say, "I forgive you; I just can't be close to you again." Consider Matthew 6:12 (see margin). How would you feel if you confessed a sin to God and He

replied, "I forgive you, but I can't be close to you again."
If you are like I am, you probably wouldn't feel forgiven.

God gives us an incredibly high standard to emulate
when we have the opportunity to forgive someone (see
Eph. 4:32). Fortunately, He also gives us the grace and
guidance we need when we imitate Him.

You Cannot Do It Alone

Be kind and compassionate to one another, forgiving each other, just as in Christ God forgave you (Eph. 4:32).

Forgiving others in your own strength, especially when
they have hurt you deeply, is impossible. You can try not
to think about what they did, stuff your feelings, or put
on a false smile when you see them. But unless God
cleanses and changes your heart, the memories will still
lurk in the background. This lingering unforgiveness will
poison your thoughts and words and can keep trust and
relationship from being rebuilt.

Only one way exists to overcome these barriers: admitting that you desperately need God to change your heart.
Often I have prayed, "God, I can't forgive in my own
strength. In fact, I do not want to forgive him, at least
until he has suffered for what he did to me. Everything in
me wants to keep a high wall up so he can't hurt me
again. But Your Word says that unforgiveness builds a
wall between you and me. You gave up your own Son in
order to forgive me. Please help me forgive and love others the way you forgave and love me."

Relying on God in this way is the key step in beginning
to forgive. God is delighted to answer this call for help.
As we receive and depend on His grace to us, we can
breathe out the grace of forgiveness to others.

What Forgiveness Is Not

To understand what forgiveness is, first look at what it is
not.

Forgiveness is not a feeling. It is an act of the will.
Forgiveness involves deciding to call on God to change

your heart. Then decide not to think or talk about what someone has done to hurt you. Make these decisions regardless of your feelings.

Second, **forgiveness is not forgetting**. Forgetting is a *passive* process in which a matter fades from memory as time passes. Forgiving is an *active* process involving a conscious choice. When God says He "remembers your sins no more" (see Isa. 43:25), He doesn't say that He *cannot* remember your sins; he promises that He *will not* remember them. He chooses not to mention, recount, or think about your sin again. For us, this may require much effort. But when we resolve to stop dwelling on an offense, painful memories usually begin to fade.

Finally, **forgiveness is not excusing**. Excusing says, "That's okay" and implies, "What you did wasn't really wrong." Forgiveness is the opposite of excusing. The fact that forgiveness is needed and granted indicates that what someone did was wrong. Forgiveness says, "We both know that what you did was wrong and without excuse. But since God has forgiven me, I forgive you." Because forgiveness deals honestly with sin, it brings a freedom that no amount of excusing could provide.

What Forgiveness Is

A woman complained to her pastor, "Every time my husband and I get into a fight, he gets historical." "You mean hysterical", her pastor replied. She responded, "No, historical. He keeps a mental record of everything I've done wrong. When he's mad, I get a history lesson." Many people bring up others' wrongs repeatedly. This pattern destroys relationships and deprives them of the peace and freedom of genuine forgiveness.

Consider these two Greek words for forgive. *Aphiemi* means to let go, release, or remit. In Scripture it often refers to debts canceled in full (see Matt. 6:12). *Charizomai* means to bestow favor freely. This word shows that forgiveness cannot be earned (see Luke 7:42-43).

I, even I, am he who blots out your transgressions, for my own sake, and remembers your sins no more (Isa. 43:25).

Forgive us our debts, as we also have forgiven our debtors (Matt. 6:12).

"Neither of them had the money to pay him back, so he canceled the debts of both. Now, which of them will love him more?" Simon replied, "I suppose the one who had the bigger debt canceled" (Luke 7:42-43).

As these words indicate, forgiveness can be costly. When someone sins, he or she creates a debt that someone must pay. Most of this debt is owed to God, who sent His Son to pay that debt on the cross for all who trust in Him (see Col. 1:19-20).

If someone sinned against you, part of his or her debt is also owed to you. You can *extract (or forcibly draw forth) payments* from that person by withholding forgiveness, being cold and aloof, lashing back, gossiping, or seeking revenge. Such actions may feel good at the time but usually cost you in the long run. I've heard people say, "Unforgiveness is the poison we drink, hoping others will die."

Or you can *make payments* on the debt and thereby release others from deserved penalties. Sometimes you decide to forgive; by God's grace you fully cancel the debt in your heart and mind. But when a deep wrong has occurred, the debt it creates is not always paid at once. This requires fighting against painful memories, speaking gracious words when you really want to say something hurtful, or enduring the consequences of a material or physical injury that the other person is unable or unwilling to repair.

If you believe in Jesus, you have more than enough to make these payments. On the cross, He already paid off the ultimate debt for sin and established an account of abundant grace in your name.

As you draw on God's grace daily, you will find that you have all you need to make the payments of forgiveness for those who have wronged you. In this manner, we forgive in exactly the way God forgives us (see Ps. 130:3-4 and 1 Cor. 13:5).

Forgiveness involves a decision to make four promises:
- I will not dwell on this incident.
- I will not bring up this incident again and use it against you.
- I will not talk to others about this incident.
- I will not let this incident stand between us or hinder our personal relationship.

For God was pleased to have all his fullness dwell in him, and through him to reconcile to himself all things, whether things on earth or things in heaven, by making peace though his blood, shed on the cross (Col. 1:19-20).

If you, O Lord, kept a record of sins, O Lord, who could stand? But with you there is forgiveness; therefore you are feared (Ps. 130:3-4).

[Love] is not rude, it is not self-seeking, it is not easily angered, it keeps no record of wrongs (1 Cor. 13:5).

By making and keeping these promises, you can tear down walls that stand between you and your offender. My wife, Corlette, summarized these four promises in a little poem for her children's curriculum, *The Young Peacemaker:* "Good thought, Hurt you not, Gossip never, Friends forever."

Many people have never understood or experienced this kind of forgiveness. When they hear the words, "I forgive you", they continue to struggle with feelings of guilt and estrangement. So when others wrong you, go beyond saying, "I forgive you"; describe the four promises that those three special words contain. Furthermore, remember that forgiveness provides an excellent opportunity to glorify God by sharing the good news of what Jesus did on the cross and how His love is the model for your forgiveness.

When Should You Forgive?

Ideally, repentance precedes forgiveness (see Luke 17:3). However, you may choose to overlook a minor offense even if the offender has not expressly repented (see Prov. 19:11).

When an offense is too serious to overlook and the offender has not yet repented, you may approach forgiveness as a two-step process. The first step, **having an attitude of forgiveness**, is unconditional and is a commitment you make to God (see Mark 11:25). Seek to maintain a loving, merciful outlook toward someone who has offended you. This requires living out the first promise of forgiveness you just read. Pray for the other person; stand ready to pursue complete reconciliation as soon as he or she repents.

The second step, **granting forgiveness**, is conditional on the offender's repentance and occurs between you and that person (see Luke 17:3-5). You commit to make the other three promises of forgiveness to the offender. When a serious offense has occurred, you cannot appropriately

If your brother sins, rebuke him, and if he repents, forgive him (Luke 17:3).

A man's wisdom gives him patience; it is to his glory to overlook an offense (Prov. 19:11).

And when you stand praying, if you hold anything against anyone, forgive him, so that your Father in heaven may forgive you your sins (Mark 11:25).

"If your brother sins, rebuke him, and if he repents, forgive him. If he sins against you seven times a day, and seven times comes back to you and says, 'I repent,' forgive him." The apostles said to the Lord, "Increase our faith!" (Luke 17:3-5).

make these promises until the offender has repented. Until then, you may need to talk with the offender about his or her sin or seek others' involvement to resolve the matter (see Matt. 18:16-20). You could not do this if you had already made the last three promises. But once the other person repents, you can make these promises, closing the matter forever, the same way that God forgives you.

Can You Ever Mention the Sin Again?

Avoid using the four promises in a rigid, mechanical fashion. Particularly, avoid using the commitment to "not bring this up again and use it against you" to prevent you from dealing realistically with recurring sin patterns.

For example, you may have forgiven someone who confessed to losing his temper. Now, he has done it again. Although you are willing to forgive him again, for his sake you may help him see that he is caught in an ongoing pattern of sin, which calls for biblical counsel. You do not bring up his past wrong to use against him but rather to benefit him. However, only bring up a past wrong again if a highly compelling reason exists to do so—not just to bolster your case against someone.

What about the Consequences?

Forgiveness does not automatically release a wrongdoer from all consequences of sin. God may allow certain consequences to remain to teach us and others not to sin again. In the Bible God forgave the Israelites for rebelling against Him in the wilderness but decreed that they would die without entering the Promised Land (Num. 14:20-23). He also forgave David for adultery and murder but did not shield him from all consequences that naturally flowed from his sin (1 Sam. 12:11-14).

You may appropriately relieve a repentant wrongdoer from at least some of his or her sin's consequences

But if he will not listen, take one or two others along, so that every matter may be established by the testimony of two or three witnesses. If he refuses to listen to them, tell it to the church; and if he refuses to listen even to the church, treat him as you would a pagan or a tax collector. I tell you the truth, whatever you bind on earth will be bound in heaven; and whatever you loose on earth will be loosed in heaven. Again I tell you that if two of you on earth agree about anything you ask for, it will be done for you by my Father in heaven. For where two or three come together in my name, there am I with them (Matt. 18:16-20).

74

(Gen. 50:15-21). If, for example, someone negligently damaged your property and cannot pay for needed repairs, you may decide to bear the cost yourself.

On the other hand, releasing a forgiven person from consequences might not be wise or loving. For example, a treasurer who secretly stole from your church may benefit from having to repay what he or she took. A careless teenager may drive more safely in the future if he or she has to pay for damages.

As you live out the four promises, ask God to help you do only what will help build up the other person.

During the Session

Introductory time (10 mins.)
1. Greet members as they arrive. Say a word of appreciation for each. Thank each for participating in the *Peacefakers, Peacebreakers, and Peacemakers* study.
2. Ask one or two volunteers to state ways in which they have already employed peacemaking concepts in their day-to-day relationships.
3. As leader open the meeting in prayer. Pray for members' continuing awareness of how they can be peacemakers in every aspect of their lives.

Group discussion (35 mins.)
4. Give a brief, three-minute overview of the sections "A High Standard" and "You Cannot Do It Alone" in today's lesson. Then ask members to turn to page 63 in the *Member Book* and answer item 1: Think of a time that you have prayed a prayer similar to the one Ken Sande prayed in the opening illustration. If you have ever prayed such a prayer—asking God to help you forgive in His strength and not in yours—describe that situation below. (As leader share an example from your own life, such as, *A very close friend once shared with others some confidential information about me. On my own strength I have*

been unable to forgive him, but through God's strength, I have forgiven.) Ask members to pair off after writing their answers. Ask each person to share with the fellow group member his or her answer. After about two minutes of sharing, ask for a volunteer willing to share his or her answer with the entire group.

5. Give a brief, two-minute summary of the section "What Forgiveness Is Not" in today's lesson. Then ask members to answer item 2: Below are listed the three statements about what forgiveness is not. Put a star by which of the three, if any, is the most surprising to you. After members have spent about a minute writing their answers, call on a volunteer to share with the class his or her response.

6. Give a two-minute overview of the section "What Forgiveness Is." Ask members to write their answers to item 3 in the *Member Book*: Describe a time you have extracted (or forcibly drawn forth) a payment from a person who sinned against you. What were the short-term consequences? the long-term consequences? After about two minutes have elapsed, call on a volunteer willing to share his or her answer.

7. Direct members to item 4 in the *Member Book*. Describe a time when God deposited in your account more than an ample amount of grace that you needed to make the payments of forgiveness for someone who wronged you. Give members about two minutes to write their answers. Then call on a volunteer to tell the group what he or she wrote.

8. Point members to item 5 in the *Member Book*, in which they are to put a star by the promise listed there that they believe is the most difficult to make in the area of forgiveness. Give them one minute to complete this activity. Then ask members to move on to item 6 and write a prayer, asking God to help them in the area they starred in item 5. Tell them that they will have the opportunity to pray that prayer in just a few minutes.

9. Ask members to look at item 7, in which they are to describe their response to the statement from the "What

Forgiveness Is" section: "Forgiveness provides an excellent opportunity to glorify God by sharing what Jesus did on the cross and how His love is the model for your forgiveness." Direct members to the item-7 questions: How do you feel when you read this statement? and Have you ever done this before—used the occasion of your forgiveness of someone as an opportunity to share about Jesus? If so, what was the outcome? Give them two minutes to answer these questions before moving on. Call on one volunteer to share his or her experience in this area.

10. Give a one-minute overview of the section "When Should You Forgive?" As you finish, direct members to item 8 in the *Member Book*. Ask them to fill in the blank words missing in the two steps to forgiveness listed there. Ask them to look up the two Scriptures listed by their blanks in item 8. Ask a volunteer to call out to the class the answers he or she wrote in the blanks.

11. Give a two-minute overview of the sections "Can You Ever Mention the Sin Again?" and "What About the Consequences?" Then direct members to item 9 in the *Member Book*, in which they are to put a check mark beside the situation(s) in which the most loving approach may well be to not release the person from the consequences of his or her sin. Ask them to form groups of three or four members to discuss their answers. Ask members whether they can think of and share illustrations in their own lives in which they saw someone grow because they did not release that person from the consequences of his or her sin. Call time after about five minutes.

12. (optional, if time allows) Show Peacemaker Parable "Forgive You?" (5 mins.). Ask members to answer questions in item 10 in the *Member Book* as they view the brief parable: How well do you think Rick did in apologizing to Andy? *Rick's apology met the elements of an adequate apology in that it was specific and sincere. He did not allow Andy to merely brush it off with an "It's no problem" reply.* How would you evaluate Andy's response in terms of the four promises that are essential elements of forgiveness?

*Andy violated all four promises: he mentioned the incident
again to Rick, his wife, and his co-worker; he said hurtful
things about Rick; he continued to dwell on it in his thoughts;
and he allowed it to interfere in his relationship with Rick.*
13. Direct members back to the prayer they wrote in
item 6 of the *Member Book,* in which they asked God to
help them in a specific area. Ask them to bow their heads
and silently pray this prayer to God.

Preview further study (1 min.)
14. Direct members to item 11 in the *Member Book* regarding further study. Encourage members who have been
completing their further study items in previous weeks to
complete this week's further-study work as well, even if
the group does not choose to continue into the second
part of the *Peacefakers, Peacebreakers, and Peacemakers* study.
Tell them that the readings, devotionals, and application
questions will make a fitting conclusion to the six-week
study or an excellent bridge for the next part of the study,
depending on the group's decision.

Closure (4 mins.)
15. Give a brief preview of the second six weeks of lessons
in *Peacefakers, Peacebreakers, and Peacemakers.* Determine
what the group's desire is regarding continuing in the
study. Assure members that you will continue to be available for them regarding their peacemaking issues regardless of whether the group decides to continue in the next
phase.
16. If the group chooses to continue, announce the time,
date, and place of the next session, if these matters apply.
If the group chooses to move on to another topic,
announce the topic if you know it. Another option is to
take a brief break, such as six weeks, between topics and
pick up part 2 of the study after this break. Although a
group would benefit most by studying part 2 just after
completing part 1, no harm would occur by spacing out
the two parts.

17. Thank members for the privilege of leading them in this course. Congratulate them on completing part 1 of *Peacefakers, Peacebreakers, and Peacemakers.* Assure them that the investment of time they have made in learning to breathe grace as peacemakers will impact them in all areas of their lives.

15. Close with prayer. Invite as many members to pray aloud spontaneously as are willing. Suggest that they thank God for walking side-by-side with them throughout the part-1 study.

After the Session

1. Evaluate the entire group experience in the *Peacefakers, Peacebreakers, and Peacemakers* study. Make a list of areas of your strengths as a leader during the group sessions. Also jot down areas in which you desire more growth. This list will help you regardless of what topic you lead in future classes.

2. Pray for class members as you remember their prayer requests. Pray that they will continue to experience growth in peacemaking skills. Thank God for the privilege you had to lead this group. If the group continues for part 2, ask God to grant you wisdom as you press on.

3. If your group chooses to continue the study without a break, read "Before the Session" for group session 1 to determine the amount of preparation you will need for the next group session. At the top of the group session 1 material in this *Leader Guide* record when you will do your preparation.

4. If your group is continuing this study, carefully study week 2 and complete all the exercises in week 2 to stay ahead of the group.

Second Six Weeks

Speak the Truth in Love

GROUP SESSION 1

Before the Session

1. Review week 1. Read and complete the lesson for week 2 to stay ahead of the group.

2. Master this week's material in the *Leader Guide.*

3. If you are using the video or DVD, arrange for a VCR or DVD player and a monitor during the session.

4. Consider calling returning members and expressing your delight that they are continuing in the study. Express your thanks for each member's participation in the part-1 study. Convey your excitement about the continued emphasis on peacemaking during part 2. Be available to answer questions that any have about either the previous or new study. This might be a good time to call members who attended infrequently during part 1 to encourage them to return for part 2, even if they weren't present for each part-1 session. Also consider calling prospects for your class. Let them know about the study that is to begin.

5. Secure copies of *Peacefakers, Peacebreakers, and Peacemakers* for newcomers who did not participate in any of the part-1 sessions.

6. Find a quiet time and place to pray for group members by name. Pray for visitors the Lord might bring to your group this week. Ask for the wisdom you need to prepare for and lead the first session of part 2.

7. Plan to stay within the given times for each activity. However, remember that allowing members to share freely as the Holy Spirit leads is more important than is sticking to a plan you develop for the group.

The Lesson
By Ken Sande
Author of *The Peacemaker*

Both Law and Gospel

Words play a key role in conflict. When properly used, words promote understanding and agreement. When misused, they drive people further apart. God can help you learn to communicate constructively.

When people disappoint or offend me, I tend to approach them with "the law"—lecturing them about what they did wrong and how they can make things right. This typically makes people defensive and reluctant to admit their wrongs, which worsens a conflict.

The Lord has taught me, instead, to bring them the gospel—the good news about what God has done and is doing for us through Christ.

The Bible provides many illustrations of how to use the gospel to set the stage for loving correction. For example, before Jesus confronted the Samaritan woman about her sin, He spent time telling her the good news of God's plan to redeem the world (John 4:7-26). The apostle Paul used a similar approach when he needed to bring correction to the Corinthians and the Colossians (1 Cor. 1:2-9; Col. 1:3-23).

As these passages show, when we need to talk with others about their faults, focus on God's goodness rather than dwelling on others' failures. Certainly we sometimes need to show them places in which they have fallen short of God's ways. But that need not be the main focus of our words, because judgment inevitably discourages. We instead can offer hope by drawing attention to the wonderful news that God forgave our sins through Christ and wants to help us change our ways.

When talking with someone about gossip, for example, you might say the following: "I don't think you deliberately set out to hurt Bill, but your words may have damaged his reputation. The good news is that Jesus died to deliver you, me, and Bill—all of us—from our sins. God has given us a warning and wonderful promise: if we conceal our wrongs, he will continue to discipline us until we repent, but if we confess our sins, he will forgive us and restore our relationships. We have such hope because of what Jesus has done for us! If you ask for His help and deal with this in the way He teaches, the whole incident can be completely resolved."

I've seen this approach open the door for repentance and peace, whether I'm doing peacemaking at home, in my church, or in a formal conciliation case. When you offer hope by focusing on what God has done, others are more likely to listen, admit their wrongs, and move toward reconciling.

Be Quick to Listen

My dear brothers, take note of this: Everyone should be quick to listen, slow to speak and slow to become angry (Jas. 1:19).

He who answers before listening— that is his folly and his shame (Prov. 18:13).

Listening carefully to others is another element of good communication (see James 1:19). Listening shows respect for the other person and shows that you are trying to understand his or her perspective. Here are a few helpful listening skills:

1. Waiting—Wait patiently while others talk. If you don't, you may fail to understand the root of a conflict and thus act inappropriately (see Prov. 18:13). Avoid jumping to premature conclusions, discipline yourself not to interrupt, do not respond the moment you hear a pause, and avoid offering immediate solutions. Often people already know what's best to do but merely need to talk it through.

2. Attending—Pay attention to what others say—maintain eye contact, avoid negative body language, eliminate distractions, lean slightly forward to show interest, and nod occasionally to show you understand. Give the other person occasional responses such as "I see" or "Hmmm."

3. Clarifying—Ask questions such as, "Are you saying
. . .?" or "Can you give me an example?", or offer comments such as, "Let me see if I understand." This may
enable you to go beyond surface issues and discern
underlying emotions more clearly.

4. Reflecting—This involves summarizing the other
person's main points; it may deal with both the content
and the feelings that the other person has expressed.
Examples include, "You felt hurt by my comment about
you in front of the class"; "You must really care about this
project"; "I get the impression I've really disappointed
you." Reflecting doesn't require that you agree with the
other person but merely reveals your effort to understand
others.

5. Agreeing—You acknowledge what you know is true
before you address points of disagreement. Examples
include: "You're right. I was wrong when I said . . ." and
"I can understand why you would be upset with my
being late again." First, resist defending yourself and
blaming others. Ask yourself, "Does any truth exist in
what he or she says?" If so, identify common ground
before you move to your differences (see Prov. 15:31).

He who listens to a life-giving rebuke will be at home among the wise (Prov. 15:31).

These five responses require having genuine humility
and keeping a tight rein on your emotions. But they are
worth the effort. A controlled response usually does more
for peace than does a thoughtless, emotional reaction (see
Prov. 15:28).

The heart of the righteous weighs its answers, but the mouth of the wicked gushes evil (Prov. 15:28).

The Tongue of the Wise Brings Healing

Good communication also involves speaking to others in a
clear, constructive, and persuasive manner (see Prov. 12:18).
Learning to use the following skills will help you speak
this way:

Reckless words pierce like a sword, but the tongue of the wise brings healing (Prov. 12:18).

1. Breathing grace—We breathe in and are filled with
God's grace through studying and meditating on His
Word, prayer, worship, thanking Him, and fellowshipping with other believers. Then we can "breathe out"

grace to others by confessing our wrongs, forgiving, lovingly showing them their faults, and bringing them hope through the gospel.

Love does not delight in evil but rejoices with the truth. It always protects, always trusts, always hopes, always perseveres (1 Cor. 13:6-7).

2. Making charitable judgments—Believe the best about others until you have facts to prove otherwise. If two ways exist to interpret what someone has done, God calls you to embrace the positive interpretation until facts prove otherwise (see 1 Cor. 13:6-7).

3. Speaking the truth in love—Ask God to put a love into your heart that is not naturally there (1 Cor. 13:1-7). Ask Him to help you communicate this love by speaking to others gently and patiently and by showing genuine concern for their well-being and interests (see Phil. 2:3-4). When a firmer manner is required, especially if others refuse to pay attention to a gentle approach, do so in a loving spirit (see 1 Thess. 5:14-15). Strong words are more likely to evoke defensiveness.

Do nothing out of selfish ambition or vain conceit, but in humility consider others better than yourselves (Phil. 2:3-4).

4. Helping others examine the desires of their hearts—Start by humbly describing the idols you have found in your own heart (see week 3) and confess how these have caused you to sin in this conflict or in others. If the person seems receptive, graciously suggest that perhaps good desires have gripped his or her heart too strongly as well. Recommend that the person ask him or her the "X-ray" questions referred to in chapter 3. Although telling someone what goes on in his or her own heart is impossible, your example can encourage others to examine their own hearts.

And we urge you, brothers, warn those who are idle, encourage the timid, help the weak, be patient with everyone. Make sure that nobody pays back wrong for wrong, but always try to be kind to each other and to everyone else (1 Thess. 5:14-15).

5. Choosing the right time and place—If possible, avoid discussing sensitive matters with someone who is tired, is worried about other things, or is in a bad mood, or when you are short on time. Avoid talking in front of others about such matters. Find a distraction-free spot or a place, such as home, in which the person will feel secure.

6. Talking from beside, not from above—Avoid talking down to the person, as though you are faultless and the person is inferior. Tell how you have wrestled with the same or other sins; give hope by describing how God has forgiven you and is working to help you change.

7. Talking in person whenever possible—Face-to-face conversation is usually better than talking by telephone. Seeing facial expressions and body language is important. Letters may help if the other person declines to respond to personal conversations or phone calls. Write as personally and graciously as possible; use your writing to invite communication. If possible, set aside a letter's first draft for a day or two and check it again for harmful words before you mail it. The same is true for emails, which often are written in the heat of immediate emotions.

8. Engaging rather than declaring—Bluntly announcing someone's faults often makes the person defensive and retaliatory. Instead open a conversation in a way that shows genuine concern for the other person. Jesus, a master at this, used stories and metaphors (such as Luke 10:25-37. See also 2 Sam. 12:1-13.) to touch people's hearts. Similarly, when my son has failed to do his chores, I often talk to him using a military metaphor, since he admires soldiers. Try to capture others' attention or appeal to their values rather than bluntly declaring their wrongs.

9. Planning your words—In delicate situations, careful planning can make the difference between restored peace or increased hostility (see Prov. 14:22b). Consider writing out issues to discuss, words or topics to avoid, analogies or metaphors that others will understand, words that describe your feelings, the effect the problem has on you and others, your suggestions for a solution, and benefits to others by cooperating. Respond to anger with a gentle voice, relaxed posture, and calm gestures.

Those who plan what is good find love and faithfulness (Prov. 14:22b).

10. Using "I" statements—A "you" message ("You made me so mad when you . . ..") invites defensiveness and counterattack. Instead, give information about yourself. Say, "I feel hurt when you make fun of me in front of other people . . .." If someone understands the behavior's effect on you, the person may be more willing to discuss and deal with the problem.

11. Being objective—Avoid subjective opinions and judgments; use objective facts if possible. Avoid words such as "you always","you never", and "every time." Exaggerations keep people from taking you seriously.

12. Using the Bible carefully—Use it only to build others up in the Lord, not to tear others down or "preach" to them. Rather than quoting Scripture to people, ask them to read a helpful passage from their own Bible and tell you what they think it means.

13. Asking for feedback—To insure that what you meant to say has been communicated completely and accurately, ask for clarification, such as, "I'm not sure I've said this clearly. Would you mind telling me what you think I said?" This will help you measure how the other person is responding to you.

14. Offering solutions and preferences—Showing a person a reasonable way out of a predicament may prompt cooperation. For example, "My first choice would be to get the whole family together to discuss Dad's will in person. What do you think?" Promote dialogue and reasonable thinking to keep people from remaining entrenched in one position.

15. Recognizing your limits—You can raise concerns, suggest solutions, and encourage reasonable thinking, but you can't force others to change. Only God can actually bring about repentance (see 2 Tim. 2:24-26). God calls us to be faithful, not to achieve results. He will honor our efforts in *His* way and in *His* time.

And the Lord's servant must not quarrel; instead, he must be kind to everyone, able to teach, not resentful. Those who oppose him he must gently instruct, in the hope that God will grant them repentance leading them to knowledge of the truth, and that they will come to their senses and escape from the trap of the devil, who has taken them captive to do his will (2 Tim. 2:24-26).

During the Session

Introductory time (10 mins.)

1. Greet members as they arrive. Tell participants how pleased you are that they have chosen to study part 2 of the *Peacefakers, Peacebreakers, and Peacemakers.* Consider making nametags for this kickoff session, especially if new group members have been added.

2. Begin promptly. Take a few minutes to recap the basic principles of the part-1 study. Encourage members that they will benefit from the part-2 study even if they were unable to participate in part 1.

3. Ask volunteers among the returning members to share one life change that has occurred since they began the entire study. This is a good opportunity to reflect on victories or challenges that have occurred during the preceding days as well as to refresh members' memories about the major emphases of the earlier studies. Stop and pray as the group embarks on the new study. Ask God to prepare members' hearts for how He wants them to be peacemakers in every aspect of their lives.

Group discussion (35 mins.)

4. Give a brief, three-minute overview of the section "Both Law and Gospel" in today's lesson. As you give the overview, delay giving specific details about how the Bible characters dealt with conflict because members will give reports on this in the following exercise. Then ask members to turn to page 77 in the *Member Book*. Direct them to item 1. Divide members into four groups. Assign each group one of the passages listed under item 1. Ask group members to study the passage assigned and to determine how the speaker or writer in the passage set a positive context for correction. *(Answer: by focusing first on what God has done and is doing for us through Christ.)* Allow groups about five minutes to work on their answers. Ask one person from each group to give a report. Suggest that members fill in the blanks under item 1 as each group reports.

5. Give a two-minute review of the section, "Be Quick to Listen." Direct members to item 2 in the *Member Book*. Ask them to match the listening skill in the left-hand column with the correct example of it in the right-hand column. Ask them to then put a star beside the skill that is the easiest for them to do and a check mark by the one most difficult for them. (Answers: e,1; b,2; a,3; c,4; d,5)

6. Give a two-minute review of the first five points in the section "The Tongue of the Wise Brings Healing."

(Breaking these sections up into smaller segments helps listeners retain more information.) Have members to turn to item 3 in the *Member Book* and ask them to think about the five skills you just shared with them. Under item 3 ask them to describe a time in which they used one of the five skills in an effort to resolve a conflict. After giving them about one minute to write their answer, call on a volunteer to share with the group his or her response.

7. Give a two-minute review of the second five points in the section "The Tongue of the Wise Brings Healing." Direct members to item 4—the three case studies of individuals using skills you just mentioned. Ask members to write the name of the skill that each person used in the blank next to each case study. (Answers: 1. *using "I" statements;* 2. *talking in person whenever possible;* 3. *planning your words.)*

8. Give a two-minute review of the remaining five points in the section "The Tongue of the Wise Brings Healing." Direct members to item 5 in the *Member Book.* Of the skills just mentioned, ask them to indicate which one the speaker in each example fails to use or uses improperly. (Answers: 1. *being objective;* 2. *recognizing your limits,* 3. *using the Bible carefully)*

9. (optional, if time allows) Show Peacemaker Parable "Word Pictures" (9 mins.). Ask members to answer questions in item 6 in the *Member Book* as they view the brief parable: How successful was Janet in using word pictures to describe her feelings about her marriage to Jim? Would some other approach have been more effective? *Jim didn't like Janet's word picture about the gazebo, the home, and the office building. Perhaps Janet could have communicated more effectively if she also had used an "I" message, linking it to her feelings. This would have been less accusatory and would have provided Jim information about her.* Which of the communications skills you have learned in this week-1 study did Janet and Jim fail to use in working out their conflict? *Jim failed to be objective. He used "you never." Janet failed to engage rather than declare. She began her remarks by*

expressing her bitterness rather than expressing concern for Jim, but it did help Jim to understand more accurately how she felt about their relationship. She could have chosen a better time and place for the discussion rather than at bedtime at the end of a long day, when Jim was not at his best. What skills could have kept the issues between Jim and Janet resolved on a day-to-day basis instead of allowing them to build up over a five-year period? *Clearly the issues in Jim and Janet's marriage were not taken care of as they developed. Jim had never told Janet about the hurt and embarrassment he felt when he lost his job or his heartbreak over the statements she made about his washing dishes while unemployed. She apparently had never communicated to him about how lonely she felt over his preoccupation with work. Jim indicated he was not in the habit of telling Janet he loved her; she indicated that he had not been open to her love during the past five years.* Ask them to fill in the blanks: Years of peace-_faking_ exploded in a fit of peace-_breaking_ but were finally resolved by genuine peace-_making_. *Processing individual issues as they occur and learning to use "I" messages at the time would have helped greatly in this marriage. All of the skills we studied could have helped them in some way at the right time instead of letting things fester.* Call on volunteers to share their answers with the group.

10. Ask members to pair up for a time of prayer (about three minutes). Ask each member to disclose to his or her partner an area in which the Holy Spirit may have prompted the person to change his or her approach to dealing with conflict as the lesson was taught. Call on members to pray for each other specifically in these areas in which growth is needed.

Preview further study (2 mins.)

11. Direct members to item 7 in the *Member Book* regarding further study. Explain that the extra work for this week involves reading from *The Peacemaker*, reading the five daily devotionals (adapted from *The Peacemaker*), and completing "If You Are Presently Involved in a Conflict."

Closure (3 mins.)
12. Thank members for a good first session of the new term of study. Assure them that you look forward to future weeks of fellowship and learning with them. Encourage members to pray for each other during the week. Ask them to pray for you as you endeavor to lead the group. Call on a volunteer to offer a prayer of dismissal.

After the Session

1. Pray about the events that transpired during the session just concluded. Thank God for His activity in the midst of the session. Ask the Holy Spirit to continue to stir each member's heart during the week ahead, so each can practically apply the lessons learned.
2. Use the following questions to evaluate your leadership:
   * Was I thoroughly prepared?
   * Was my presentation clear?
   * Did I follow the *Leader Guide*?
   * Did I provide positive leadership?
   * Was I a servant leader?
   * Did I create a healthy group environment?
   * Did I help members communicate with each other?
   * Do members understand the purpose of the study?
   * Was I enthusiastic about how God will use *Peacefakers, Peacebreakers, and Peacemakers* in the life of our church?
3. Read group session 2 to determine the amount of preparation you will need for the next group session. At the top of the group session 2 material in this *Leader Guide* record when you will do your preparation.
4. Carefully study week 3 and complete all the exercises to stay ahead of the group.

Take One or Two Others Along

GROUP SESSION 2

Before the Session

1. Review week 2. Read and complete the lesson for week 3 to stay ahead of the group. Since some of the concepts in this week's lesson are complicated and controversial, a leader would be wise to read carefully before class pages 185-199 in *The Peacemaker*.
2. Master this week's material in the *Leader Guide*.
3. If you are using the video or DVD, arrange for a VCR or DVD player and a monitor during the session.
4. Consider calling visitors from last week's meeting and letting them know they are welcome to return. Also consider calling irregular attenders (during part 1) who may have been present during last week's session. Encourage them to return and to continue in the *Peacefakers, Peacebreakers, and Peacemakers* study.
5. Plan to stay within the given times for each activity.

The Lesson
By Ken Sande
Author of *The Peacemaker*

The Matthew 18 Process

We've seen that the Bible encourages Christians to make every effort to resolve their differences as personally and privately as possible. If we draw on God's grace and follow the principles He gives us in Scripture, we can resolve most conflicts on our own. Sometimes, however, we need help from other people. Having someone else act as an intermediary before we even try to talk with another person sometimes will speed reconciliation. In other cases we may need to ask one or more respected friends, church leaders, or other godly, unbiased individuals to act as mediators or arbitrators. (See The Slippery Slope, p. 4.)

In Matthew 18:15-20 Jesus sets forth the framework for seeking others' help to solve a conflict. In this passage, Jesus shows how to minister to a fellow Christian who is caught in sin. Since prolonged conflict usually involves sin (see Jas. 4:1), this passage directly applies to peacemaking. Today we will walk through this process step by step and see how you can apply it as you seek to restore someone to a right relationship with God and others. (Although Matthew 18 applies specifically to disputes between Christians, the general concepts also can work well with non-Christians.)

What causes fights and quarrels among you? Don't they come from your desires that battle within you? (Jas. 4:1).

Matthew 18 teaches generally that we try to keep the circle of people involved in a conflict as small as possible for as long as possible. If you can resolve a dispute personally and privately, do so. But if you cannot settle matters on your own, seek others' help. Whenever you cannot deal with a problem or conflict on your own, the body of Christ can guide and assist you.

Step One: Overlook Minor Offenses

Therefore, if you are offering your gift at the altar and there remember that your brother has something against you, leave your gift there in front of the altar. First go and be reconciled to your brother; then come and offer your gift (Matt. 5:23-24).

Before you consider involving others in a conflict, review the steps that you can take to resolve a dispute in private. Evaluate how you can use the situation as an opportunity to glorify God, serve others, and grow to be like Christ (see part 1, session 2). Then consider resolving the dispute unilaterally by overlooking minor offenses and giving up certain personal rights (see part 1, sessions 1 and 3).

Step Two: Talk in Private

If you have wronged someone else, God calls you to go to the other person to seek forgiveness (see Matt. 5:23-24) (see part 1, sessions 1 and 4). If another person has committed a wrong that is too serious to overlook, go to that other person and point out his or her fault (see Matt. 18:15). Make every effort to resolve personal issues and promote genuine reconciliation (see part 1, sessions 5 and 6). Seek godly advisers who can help you see your own faults clearly and respond to the other person wisely.

If repeated efforts to resolve the matter in these private ways fail, and if the matter is too serious to overlook, proceed to the next step in the Matthew 18 process.

As you proceed through the Matthew 18 process, please note the "bookends of love." Verses 13-14 and 21-35, as well as the various references to "winning a brother over", show that the main purpose of the process is to lovingly restore someone who is caught in sin and who needs help being restored to others.

Step Three: Take One or Two Others Along

If a dispute cannot be resolved in private, Jesus tells us to ask other people to get involved (see Matt. 18:16). Paul gives the same instruction (see Phil. 4:2-3). Outside people can become involved in a dispute in two ways:

1. By mutual agreement. If you and your opponent cannot resolve a dispute privately, suggest that the two of you ask one or more unbiased persons to meet with you to facilitate more productive dialogue. These people, to whom I will refer as "reconcilers", may be mutual friends, church leaders, godly and respected community individuals, or trained Christian mediators or arbitrators.

Although reconciler training can help, reconcilers do not have to be professionally trained to serve in personal disputes. What is most important is that they are wise, spiritually mature, trustworthy Christians. If your dispute involves technical issues, one or more of the reconcilers may need expertise in that area.

If your opponent balks at involving others, explain why doing so would help. If the person is a Christian, refer to Matthew 18:15-20 and 1 Corinthians 6:1-8 as the biblical basis for your suggestion. With both Christians

If your brother sins against you, go and show him his fault, just between the two of you. If he listens to you, you have won your brother over (Matt. 18:15).

But if he will not listen, take one or two others along, "so that every matter may be established by the testimony of two or three witnesses" (Matt. 18:16).

I plead with Euodia and I plead with Syntyche to agree with each other in the Lord. Yes, and I ask you, loyal yokefellow, help these women who have contended at my side in the cause of the gospel, along with Clement and the rest of my fellow workers, whose names are in the book of life. (Phil. 4:2-3).

and non-Christians, you can describe the practical benefits of mediation: saving time, money, and energy (when compared to formal, legal processes); avoiding publicity; and receiving the benefit of others' experience and creativity.

2. On your initiative. While mutual agreement is preferable, Matthew 18:16 indicates that you may seek help from reconcilers even if a Christian opponent refuses to cooperate. Before you take that step, warn your opponent by saying something such as, "Bob, I prefer to resolve this matter just between the two of us. Since that has not happened and since this involves issues too important to walk away from, my only option is to obey what Jesus commands. This means asking some people from our church(es) to help us out. I prefer that we go together for that help, but if you will not cooperate, I'll ask for it myself." Sometimes such a statement will help "Bob" change his mind.

If a Christian opponent does not cooperate, you and the reconciler may personally visit the other person and ask to talk. If you believe this approach would seriously offend your opponent, the reconciler could talk to your opponent individually to try to set up a later meeting with you and the reconciler. You also may contact the other person's church and ask one of its leaders to help. A pastor or elder could accompany you or talk to your opponent privately to set up a joint meeting.

Avoid giving a reconciler unnecessary details about the conflict. Just explain that you and the other person are at odds and need help. Too much detail might cause the other party to think that you have tried to bias the reconciler in your favor. Explain in detail your perceptions only when you, the other person, and the reconciler all are present. A letter asking a reconciler to help may be best.

What do reconcilers do? They help you and your opponent decide how to restore peace. They may simply help both sides listen more carefully to each other. They may ask appropriate questions, help you and the other person get added facts, and advise you on how to deal with the problem. They may direct you to relevant Scriptural principles, encourage repentance and confession by pointing out behavior inconsistent with biblical teachings, and draw on their own knowledge to propose practical solutions. You and your opponent may agree that if you can't reach a voluntary solution, you will abide by the reconcilers' counsel. Or you may make the agreement legally binding—where reconcilers become arbitrators and render a decision that a civil court can enforce.

Step Four: Tell It to the Church (Church Accountability)

If your opponent is a professing Christian who refuses to listen to the reconcilers' counsel, and the matter is too serious to overlook, Jesus commands you to "tell it to the church" (see Matt. 18:17a). This does not mean broadcasting the conflict in a worship service. Instead, inform the other person's church leaders (and probably yours as well) of the problem. Ask them for help in promoting justice and peace by holding both of you accountable to God's Word and to your commitments.

Church leaders may consult with the reconcilers and confirm their counsel. Or they may conduct an entirely separate investigation and give their own counsel. The church's decision is intended to be binding on its own member, whether or not the party likes it. As indicated in Matthew 18:18-20 the church speaks with the authority of Christ Himself when it acts according to its biblical mandate to deal with sin. A Christian may properly disobey his or her church only when its instructions are clearly contrary to Scriptural teaching (see Matt. 23:1-3).

Step Five: Treat Him as a Nonbeliever

If the person refuses to listen to the church's counsel to repent of this sin, Jesus tells us what to do next

If he refuses to listen to them, tell it to the church (Matt. 18:17a).

Then Jesus said to the crowds and to his disciples: "The teachers of the law and the Pharisees sit in Moses' seat. So you must obey them and do everything they tell you. But do not do what they do, for they do not practice what they preach (Matt. 23:1-3).

If he refuses to listen even to the church, treat him as you would a pagan or a tax collector (Matt. 18:17b).

(see Matt. 18:17b). The church can't decide whether the person is a believer; only God knows one's heart. But if someone behaves as a nonbeliever would—by disregarding the authority of Scripture and of Christ's church—the person should be treated as if he or she were a nonbeliever.

The church should not pretend that things are fine with people who claim to be Christians yet refuse to listen to God as He speaks through the Scriptures and the church. Therefore, the church may withdraw various membership privileges, such as taking communion, holding church office, or teaching Sunday school. Revoking the person's membership status may be the ultimate outcome if he or she refuses to repent of sin. This is not done to injure people but to help them realize the seriousness of their sin.

The church should also seek every chance to evangelize such persons. We repeatedly remind them of the Good News of salvation through Jesus Christ and urge them to turn from their sin. If they behave disruptively, the church may exclude them from church gatherings and activities. Otherwise, welcome them to Sunday worship as you do other nonbelievers. But avoid talking to them in superficial ways; graciously and repeatedly remind them of their need for repentance.

Many Christians balk at this teaching. But by ignoring it, a church not only disobeys Jesus' specific commands, it also fails to face up to sin's serious consequences (Ezek. 34:4, 8-10). As Dietrich Bonhoeffer writes, "Nothing is so cruel as the tenderness that consigns another to his sin. Nothing can be more compassionate than the severe rebuke that calls a brother back from the path of sin."[1]

During the Session

Introductory time (10 mins.)
1. Be available to greet members as they arrive. Distribute copies of the *Peacefakers, Peacebreakers, and Peacemakers Member Book* to anyone who does not have a copy already.

2. Call on members to volunteer prayer requests. As leader pray for the needs mentioned. Ask members to keep the group updated on answers to prayer.

3. Direct members to item 1 in week 2 of the *Member Book*. Ask each member to write down the name or initials of a godly, wise person in the church whom you would trust to help you resolve a conflict. Tell members that this week's lesson will help them think about occasions in which they may need to rely on mature Christians in the church to serve as mediators or arbitrators.

4. Referring to the personal peacemaking portion of The Slippery Slope diagram on page 4, give a two-minute summary of the sections, "The Matthew 18 Process" and the sections that review the first two steps of the process (except for the last paragraph on lovingly restoring others.) Remind members who did not attend the first six weeks' study of *Peacefakers, Peacebreakers, and Peacemakers* that they can learn more about some of the concepts addressed in the first two steps by completing the "For Further Study" in weeks 1 and 4 (of part 1), if they desire. Ask students to read Matthew 18:12-15 and 21-22 and then answer the question in item 2, What is the main purpose of the process Jesus sets forth in verses 15-20? *(Answer: to lovingly restore a brother or sister who is caught in a sin and who needs help being restored to others.)*

5. Give a two-minute summary of "By mutual agreement" and "On your initiative" in the section "Step Three: Take One or Two Others Along." Direct members to item 3 in the *Member Book*. Ask them to look up 1 Corinthians 6:5 and Galatians 6:1, as indicated in the *Member Book*. Ask them to write down characteristics of a reconciler that these Scriptures seem to indicate. (Answers: *1 Cor. 6:5—wise; Gal. 6:1—spiritual, discerning, able to withstand temptation.)* Ask members to share their answers with the group.

6. Ask members to turn their attention to item 4 in the *Member Book*. Before you summarize the topic about what reconcilers do, ask members to write in their books what types of tasks a reconciler might perform. Give members about one minute to answer. Then ask volunteers to call

out their suggestions about what is involved in being a reconciler. Confirm answers that are correct; mention any other task that the topic in the lesson suggests.

7. Give a one-minute summary of the section, "Tell It to the Church (Church Accountability)", reviewing everything except the statement regarding a time in which a Christian may properly disobey his or her church. Members will cover this material in item 5 of the *Member Book*. Then direct members to item 5 of the *Member Book*. Ask them to look up the two passages listed in item 5 (Acts 4:18-20 and 5:27-32) and write the answers to the question: According to these passages, when may a Christian properly disobey his or her church when a church has made a final decision in a reconciliation situation? After giving members three minutes to look these up, ask a volunteer to call out the answer. (*A Christian may properly disobey his or her church only when its instructions are contrary to Scriptural teaching.*)

8. Give a two-minute summary of the section, "Treat Him as a Nonbeliever." Ask members to form groups of four or five members each. Write on a marker board or piece of newsprint these questions: "What is your reaction to this means of dealing with conflict—treat him as a nonbeliever? Has anyone in the group ever been a part of a church in which such a situation has arisen? What do you think of the premise that to ignore a member's flagrant, unrepentant sins, a church not only disobeys Jesus' specific commands but also fails to face up to sin's serious consequences?" Tell members that they can use the space provided in item 6 of the *Member Book* to take notes on their reactions. After you have allowed groups about five to seven minutes to discuss their answers to these questions, ask members to return to the large group. Ask volunteers to discuss comments they made during the small-group time.

9. (optional, if time allows) Show Peacemaker Parable "Virtual Confrontation" (5 mins.). Ask members to answer the question in item 7 in the *Member Book*: What was the

main point of the parable? *Most people do not like to confront others, or they completely misunderstand that the main point of Matthew 18:15-20 is to lovingly, personally restore a brother to a right relationship with others. To avoid this failure, we can ask God to help us obey His word faithfully whenever we see a need to correct another person.*

10. To reinforce the basic structure of Matthew 18:15-20, ask members to fill in the blanks of item 8 of the *Member Book*.

Preview further study (1 min.)

11. Direct members to item 9 in the *Member Book* regarding optional further study. Explain that the extra work for this week involves reading from *The Peacemaker*, reading the five daily devotionals (adapted from *The Peacemaker*), and completing "If You Are Presently Involved in a Conflict."

Closure (4 mins.)

12. Thank members for their participation in today's session. Express your desire to be available to them during the week if they have questions about the study.

13. For the closing prayer, ask volunteers to thank God for revealing to them some area of needed growth.

After the Session

1. Recall prayer requests and pray for each member.

2. Read group session 3 to determine the amount of preparation you will need for the next group session. At the top of the group session 3 material in this *Leader Guide* record when you will do your preparation.

3. Carefully study week 4 and complete all the exercises to stay ahead of the group.

[1]Dietrich Bonhoeffer, *Life Together*, trans. John W. Doberstein (New York: Harper & Row, 1954), 107.

Overcoming Unforgiveness

GROUP SESSION 3

Before the Session

1. Review week 3. Read and complete the lesson for
week 4 to stay ahead of the group.
2. Master this week's material in the *Leader Guide*.
3. If you are using the video or DVD, arrange for a VCR or
DVD player and a monitor during the session.
4. Contact as many of your regular members as possible to
express interest in them and their prayer requests. Let
them know how much you appreciate their faithfulness to
the group. Also call visitors or irregular attenders to
encourage them to continue in the study. Assure them
they will be blessed by attending the remaining sessions in
Peacefakers, Peacebreakers, and Peacemakers.
5. Plan to stay within the given times for each activity.
However, remember that allowing members to share
freely is more important than is sticking to a plan you
develop for the group session. Be sensitive to the Holy
Spirit's work in your group.

The Lesson
By Ken Sande
Author of *The Peacemaker*

Keeping Tough Promises

We know the importance of forgiving those who have
wronged us. But a promise of forgiveness can be difficult

to keep. Fortunately, God promises to help us forgive others. Throughout the Bible He gives many examples of personal forgiveness. The Holy Spirit gives us power to forgive others. For times when we need extra help, God provides pastors and fellow believers to counsel and encourage. As you draw on these resources, you can take these six steps to overcome unforgiveness.

1. Confirm Repentance

Forgiving someone who has failed to repent and confess clearly and specifically may be difficult. This can happen when the individual mutters, "I'm sorry", in a rather flip and rote manner. When this happens you may need to ask for an opportunity to discuss the situation further and explain specifically in what ways his or her action hurt you.

You also may need to encourage the person to take repentance more seriously. Doing this actually is a service to the person who wronged you as well as a way to help remove your own barrier to forgiveness.

2. Renounce Sinful Attitudes and Expectations

Sometimes—either consciously or unconsciously—we withhold forgiveness because we want the offender to earn it, because we want him or her to suffer, or because we want to ensure that the person won't hurt us again.

Such attitudes and expectations are inconsistent with the command to forgive as God forgave us. We can never earn or deserve God's forgiveness—that's why it is a free gift (see Rom. 6:23). Neither does God withhold forgiveness in order to punish people. Our heartfelt confession is all God wants to hear (see 1 John 1:9). Furthermore, God forgives us based on repentance, not on guarantees (see Luke 17:3-4).

We are not to let our fears about future conduct keep us from granting forgiveness. If someone repents but keeps on offending, we may talk with him or her about *present* conduct and a pattern of sinful behavior. But that gives us no right to withhold pardon from a repentant person.

For the wages of sin is death, but the gift of God is eternal life in Christ Jesus our Lord (Rom. 6:23).

If we confess our sins, he is faithful and just and will forgive our sins and purify us from all unrighteousness (1 John 1:9).

If your brother sins, rebuke him, and if he repents, forgive him. If he sins against you seven times in a day, and seven times comes back to you and says, "I repent," forgive him (Luke 17:3-4).

3. Assess Your Contributions to the Problem

Sometimes a self-righteous attitude can retard forgiveness. Even if you did not start the dispute, your lack of understanding, careless words, or failure to respond lovingly may have aggravated the situation. You may act as though the other person's sins more than cancel yours. Overcome this tendency by prayerfully examining your role in the conflict. Write down everything you have done that may have been a factor. Remembering your failure may make forgiving others easier.

4. Recognize that God Is Working for Good

When you perceive that God is actually using the person who has wronged you as an instrument to help you mature, serve others, and glorify Him, you may forgive more easily. God is sovereign; He sees the bigger picture. He may use the conflict to expose weaknesses in you or to grow you in character. Such realization may soften your heart and move you along in forgiveness.

5. Remember God's Forgiveness

Focusing on how much God has forgiven you can help you overcome unforgiveness. One way to do this is to read the parable in Matthew 18:21-35. Like the unmerciful servant, we sometimes take God's forgiveness for granted while stubbornly withholding forgiveness from others. We act as though others' sins against us are more serious than are our sins against God! This demeans what Jesus did for us on the cross. This sinful attitude will separate us from God.

To overcome these sinful attitudes, think about some specific sins for which God has forgiven you. Have you ever treated others the same way that the person you need to forgive has treated you? What do you deserve from God because of your sins? Rejoice in the words of Psalm 103:8-11 and Romans 5:8 (see them in the margin). The more you appreciate the wonders of God's forgive-

The Lord is compassionate and gracious, slow to anger, abounding in love. He will not always accuse, nor will he harbor his anger forever; he does not treat us as our sins deserve or repay us according to our iniquities. For as high as the heavens are above the earth, so great is his love for those who fear him (Ps. 103:8-11).

But God demonstrates His own love for us in this: While we were still sinners, Christ died for us (Rom. 5:8).

ness, the more you'll be motivated to forgive. And the more you forgive others, the more you will enjoy God and his marvelous forgiveness for you!

6. Draw on God's Strength

Forgiving others is impossible in your own strength. But if you ask God to change your heart and continually rely on His grace, you can forgive even the most painful offenses. Many people know the remarkable story of Corrie ten Boom. The Nazis imprisoned her with her family for aiding Jews during World War II. Her father and sister died as a result of their brutal imprisonment. Years later, God enabled Corrie to forgive one of her captors when, during a church service, she encountered the man. Corrie realized that God's grace, not her own abilities, brought about true forgiveness, even in seemingly impossible situations.

Reconciliation and Replacement Principle

Forgiveness is both an event and a process. The event takes place when we make the four promises of forgiveness that we discussed in lesson 6: I will not dwell on this incident; I will not bring up this incident again and use it against you; I will not talk to others about this incident; and I will not let this incident stand between us or hinder our personal relationship. The event of making these promises knocks down the wall standing between you and the person who wronged you. Then a process begins. The Bible calls this "reconciliation." It involves a changed attitude that leads to relationship change—what Jesus had in mind in Matthew 5:24 (see the margin).

First go and be reconciled to your brother; then come and offer your gift (Matt. 5:24).

Being reconciled with someone doesn't mean that the person now becomes your best friend, but ideally your relationship will be as good as it was before the offense occurred. Sometimes an even better relationship develops between the two of you. You may discover a growing

If your brother sins, rebuke him, and if he repents, forgive him. If he sins against you seven times in a day, and seven times comes back to you and says, "I repent", forgive him (Luke 17:3-4).

Finally, brothers, whatever is true, whatever is noble, whatever is right, whatever is pure, whatever is lovely, whatever is admirable—if anything is excellent or praiseworthy—think about such things (Phil. 4:8).

Now, instead, you ought to forgive and comfort him, so that he will not be overwhelmed by excessive sorrow. I urge you, therefore, to reaffirm your love for him (2 Cor. 2:7-8).

respect for each other. You also may uncover common interests and goals.

Reconciliation requires that you give a repentant person the chance to regain your trust. This may be slow and difficult, especially if the person has been irresponsible. While you may act cautiously, avoid demanding guarantees from a repentant person. If the person stumbles, you may need to repeat the loving confrontation, confession, and forgiveness process through setbacks (see Luke 17:3-4).

Unless you make a deliberate effort to restore and strengthen a relationship, it usually deteriorates. Unless you take definite steps to demonstrate your forgiveness, the other person may doubt you are sincere and may withdraw from you. One way to aid forgiveness is to practice the "replacement principle." You can do this at three levels:

1. In Thought

Painful thoughts about what others have done to hurt you easily pop back into your mind—even after you forgive. Instead of simply trying to stop thinking unpleasant thoughts, *replace* negative memories with positive ones. When you're tempted to brood, ask God to help you. Pray deliberately for that person. Try to think of something good about the offender. Then other positive thoughts may crop up. If you can't recall a single good thing about the person, then use thankful thoughts about God and His work in this situation to replace unpleasant memories (see Phil. 4:8).

2. In Word

When talking to others about the person who offended you, deliberately speak well of the person. Describe the person's redeeming qualities. Do the same as you talk to the offender. Praise, thank, or encourage! Kind words are especially important if the offender struggles with guilt or embarrassment. See what Paul told the Corinthian church about a repentant member (2 Cor. 2:7-8). As you sincerely build up the other person, both of you are likely to experience improved attitudes and feelings.

3. In Deed

Apply the replacement principle to your actions as well (see 1 John 3:18). Act as though you think well of the person; in time your actions may prompt a more loving spirit within you.

Dear children, let us not love with words or tongue but with actions and in truth (1 John 3:18).

Loving actions can communicate the reality of your forgiveness and how committed you are to reconciliation. If the person has acted untrustworthy in his or her offense to you, give that person an opportunity to demonstrate responsibility again—just as though nothing had ever happened. Your resentment may diminish as you see the look of surprise and gratitude on the face of the person who is the recipient of your trust.

Today's lesson demonstrates what forgiveness is all about. By thought, word, and deed, you can demonstrate forgiveness and rebuild relationships with people who have offended you. No matter how painful the offense, with God's help, you can imitate the forgiveness and reconciliation that Christ demonstrated on the cross. By the grace of God, you can forgive as the Lord forgave you.

During the Session

Introductory time (10 mins.)

1. Arrive early so you can greet each member as he or she arrives. Be alert to personal needs in members' lives, so you can remember to pray specifically. Begin promptly, even if the class is not entirely assembled.

2. As an introductory activity, explain to members that today's lesson is about overcoming unforgiveness and helping members move past any barriers that keep them from forgiving others. Ask members to pair off. As members work in pairs, ask each to share about a situation in which the person has found forgiving to be difficult, even after assuring the offender that he or she is forgiven. Ask them to recall what seemed to create the barrier to forgiveness. Tell members you will give them about five minutes of sharing time. After five minutes has elapsed, ask members to enter into a time of prayer. Ask each to pray aloud quietly, in pairs, that God

would help his or her partner develop a forgiving spirit in the situation mentioned.

Group discussion (35 mins.)

3. Give a 10-minute overview of the section "Keeping Tough Promises" in today's lesson. As you highlight each of the six steps to overcoming unforgiveness, direct members to item 1 in week 3 of the *Member Book*. Suggest that they take brief notes below each step listed in the *Member Book*. These notes will help them remember the various steps as they proceed to the next exercise.

4. Direct members to item 2 in the *Member Book*. Ask members to read each scenario and write the number of the step to overcoming unforgiveness that the offended person could best use in the situation to remove his or her barrier to forgiveness. Tell members you will give them five minutes to read the case studies and mark their answers. Ask volunteers to call out correct answers to the exercise. (Answers: *a,4; b,6; c,2; d,3; e,5; f,1.*) Ask whether any member would volunteer to describe a time in which he or she has been in a situation similar to that of the offended person in one of the case studies.

5. Give a one-minute overview of the section "Reconciliation and Replacement Principle" (first five paragraphs only). Direct members to item 3 in the *Member Book*. Ask them to look up the three Scriptures listed under item 3. Ask them to determine, by reading the Scriptures, what type of reconciliation each Scripture seems to indicate an offended person is to enact in order to restore and strengthen the friendship after forgiveness is granted. After giving them three minutes in which to work, call on volunteers to share their answers. Then, to expound on what they have answered, give a brief summary of the three levels of pursuing reconciliation through the replacement principle.

6. (optional, if time allows) Show Peacemaker Parable "Think on These Things" (4 mins.). Ask members to answer questions in item 4 in the *Member Book* as they view the brief parable: What replacement method did

Charlotte's co-worker recommend that she use in coping with her boss, Stephen, with whom she was furious? *He recommended that she replace angry thoughts with positive thoughts about Stephen.* What practical reason did her co-worker use for suggesting this idea to Charlotte? *He feared that her extreme anger might cost her her job.* For what spiritual reason did he recommend she do this? *He reminded her that she was a Christian and urged her to not let her temptation to hate take charge.* How successful was the co-worker in suggesting this replacement principle? *By the end of their talk, Charlotte agreed that she could look on Stephen more positively. Instead of lecturing Charlotte, the co-worker dealt with the issue with a touch of humor and definite empathy, which contributed to his success in persuading her.*

7. Direct members to item 5 in the *Member Book*. Ask them to reflect on today's lesson. Have them look back at the six steps to overcoming unforgiveness (item 1). Ask them to mark with a check the step they believe is the most difficult for them to do. Suggest that they stop and pray a silent prayer, asking God to enable them to use that step readily the next time they find themselves hanging onto unforgiveness.

Preview further study (1 min.)
8. Direct members to item 6 in the *Member Book* regarding optional further study. Explain that the extra work for this week involves reading from *The Peacemaker*, reading the five daily devotionals (adapted from *The Peacemaker*), and completing "If You Are Presently Involved in a Conflict."

Closure (4 mins.)
9. Encourage members to be present for next week's lesson on looking for others' interests. Encourage those who might be attending for the first time today not to feel frustrated because they haven't been in on other sessions. Assure them that they will be blessed by picking up with the study at this point.

10. Call for a couple of volunteers to close the group in prayer. Suggest that the volunteers pray about whatever the Lord has put on their hearts during today's lesson.

After the Session

1. Ask God to guide members as they process the information learned this week. Pray that they will have courage to assess their roles as potential reconcilers in church settings. As you pray, remember members' prayer requests.

2. Use the following questions to evaluate your leadership:
- Was I thoroughly prepared? Did I follow the leader guidelines for this session?
- Did I provide positive leadership? Was I the kind of leader 2 Timothy 2:24-25 describes?
- Did I create a group feeling during the opening minutes? Did it deepen?
- Did I help group members communicate with each other?

3. Read group session 4 to determine the amount of preparation you will need for the next group session. At the top of the group session 4 material in this *Leader Guide* record when you will do your preparation.

4. Carefully study week 5 and complete all the exercises to stay ahead of the group.

Look Also to the Interests of Others

GROUP SESSION 4

Before the Session

1. Review week 4. Read and complete the lesson for week 5 to stay ahead of the group.

2. Master this week's material in the *Leader Guide*.

3. If you are using the video or DVD, arrange for a VCR or DVD player and a monitor during the session.

4. Prepare a flip chart to use in the portion of the group discussion in which you highlight the steps in the PAUSE Process. On one sheet of the flip chart use a marker to list the activities involved in step one, "Prepare." On the second sheet use a marker to list the ways one can "Affirm relationships"—step 2 of the PAUSE Process.

5. Pray that each person who attends will be open to what God has to teach him or her in the remaining lessons of *Peacefakers, Peacebreakers, and Peacemakers*. As members move toward the conclusion of this study in a few weeks, they may feel a little sad if they have become involved on an emotional level. Ask God to bless these remaining weeks of study so that members will leave this course with all they need to be peacemakers in their daily lives.

6. Plan to stay within the given times for each activity.

The Lesson
By Ken Sande
Author of *The Peacemaker*

Material Issues

So far we have focused primarily on how to resolve personal issues (offenses) that can arise during a conflict. However, conflict also may involve material issues. Two friends may disagree on the cost of repairing damaged property. Businesspeople may interpret a contract in different ways. Neighbors may differ on whether a fence needs to be replaced and who bears the cost. Peace will be hindered until these substantive matters are settled, even if the related personal issues are resolved. This week we will study a negotiation strategy that can help you agree on material issues in a biblically faithful manner.

Cooperative vs. Competitive Negotiation

When material issues arise, many people automatically resort to a competitive style of negotiation, which is essentially a tug-of-war. This style has three major weaknesses: (1) It may not produce the best possible solution to a problem, because people are more likely to focus on surface issues and neglect root issues. It also assumes that for one side to get more, the other must get less. (2) It can consume much time and generate much frustration, since it involves successive compromises and concessions. (3) It can damage personal relationships, since it tends to be self-centered and send the message that relational matters are unimportant. The ensuing contest of wills can lead to overt intimidation, manipulation, and personal attacks.

Cooperative negotiating, on the other hand, reduces these tensions, since it emphasizes working *with* our opponents rather than *against* them. A solution beneficial to all is sought, underlying concerns and needs are addressed, complete solutions are pursued, less time and energy is wasted on defensive posturing, and more attention is paid to personal concern, thus preserving or even improving relationships.

Scripture highly commends cooperative negotiation, since the Bible repeatedly commands us to be actively concerned for the needs and well-being of others (see Phil. 2:3-4; Matt. 7:12).

Being concerned for others does not mean giving in automatically to their demands. We still are responsible for looking to our own interests (Phil. 2:4). Furthermore, Jesus calls us to be shrewd (see Matt. 10:16), which is translated *prudent, sensible, practically wise*. A wise person does not give in to others unless a valid reason exists to do so. After gathering all the relevant information and exploring creative options, a wise person works toward God-honoring solutions that benefit as many people as possible. This usually requires both sides contributing to a solution.

The PAUSE Process

I have found that a loving, wise process of cooperative negotiation generally involves five basic steps. I summarize it in this simple rule: When you need to negotiate, **PAUSE**. Pause is an acronym that stands for *Prepare, Affirm relationships, Understand interests, Search for creative solutions, and Evaluate options objectively and reasonably.*

Here's an explanation of each step.

1. Prepare
Prepare for negotiation in these ways:

    a. *Pray*. Ask God for humility, discernment, and wisdom.

    b. *Get the facts*. Read relevant documents carefully (e.g., contracts, employment manuals, letters). Talk with key witnesses. Conduct necessary research.

Do nothing out of selfish ambition or vain conceit, but in humility consider others better than yourselves. Each of you should look not only to your own interests, but also to the interests of others (Phil. 2:3-4).

So in everything, do to others what you would have them do to you, for this sums up the Law and the Prophets (Matt. 7:12).

I am sending you out as sheep among wolves. Therefore be as shrewd as snakes and as innocent as doves (Matt. 10:16).

c. *Identify issues and interests.* Try to discern the real cause of the disagreement. Carefully list the issues involved. List your interests as well as others' interests as you understand them.

d. *Study the Bible.* Clearly identify the biblical principles involved and how to put them into practice.

e. *Develop options.* Brainstorm so you can propose a few reasonable solutions to the problem. Prepare to show how each can benefit your opponent.

f. *Anticipate reactions.* Consider how your opponent may respond. Develop a response plan to each reaction.

g. *Plan an alternative to a negotiated agreement.* In advance decide what you will do if negotiations do not succeed.

h. *Select an appropriate time and place to talk.* Consider your opponent's possible preferences.

i. *Plan your opening remarks.* In particular, plan how to set a positive tone and how to encourage your opponent to open-mindedly enter into the discussions.

j. *Seek counsel.* If you have doubts about how to proceed, talk with people who can give you wise advice.

This may seem like a lot of work; it is. But you can either put your time into grumbling about a problem or put that time into carefully negotiating with others. The sooner you devote your time to planning a solution to the problem, the less time you will spend stewing over it.

2. Affirm relationships

A key to effective negotiation is to continually affirm your respect and concern for your opponent. Begin a conversation with words such as, "You're one of my closest friends. No one in town has been more kind or thoughtful toward me. Because I value our friendship, I want to find a solution to this problem." Back up these words with comparable actions, or else your opponent will see you as a flatterer and a hypocrite.

Here are some ways to demonstrate concern and respect during the negotiation process:

- *Communicate in a courteous manner.* Listen to what others say. Use words or sentences such as, "Please"; "May I explain?"; "I don't think I explained my reasons clearly."
- *Spend time on personal issues.* Try to understand your opponent's personal concerns instead of moving directly to material issues.
- *Submit to authority.* Offer clear and reasonable advice, but respect leaders' authority and support their decisions to the best of your ability.
- *Earnestly seek to understand.* Pay attention to what others think and feel. Ask sincere questions. Discuss their perceptions.
- *Look out for the interests of others.* Seek solutions that really satisfy others' needs and desires.
- *Address sin in a gracious manner.* If you must talk to others about their wrongs, use the skills described in week 5 of the first six weeks of study.
- *Allow face-saving.* Don't back others into a corner. Develop solutions that are consistent with others' values and with God's.
- *Give praise and thanks.* When someone makes a valid point or a gracious gesture, acknowledge it or express your appreciation for it.

Even if, at the end of the negotiation process, you are not totally satisfied with the agreement, affirm your relationship with the other person. This protects your relationship from residual damage and may improve your ability to negotiate subsequent issues more favorably.

3. Understand interests
Interests differ from issues or positions. An *issue* is an identifiable and concrete question to be addressed in order to reach an agreement. *Is it right for you to to park in front of my house?* A *position* is a desired outcome or a definable perspective on an issue. *I can park wherever I*

want! An *interest* is what motivates people—a concern, desire, need, limitation, or something that a person values. Interests provide the basis for positions. *Your car blocks my view as I back out of my driveway. Last week I nearly ran over your daughter on her bicycle.* Even when two parties' positions clash, often their interests may be surprisingly compatible. For example, both parties in this illustration are interested in the safety of the neighbor's daughter. Focusing on interests rather than positions often yields more acceptable solutions.

The Bible story of David, Nabal, and Abigail (read 1 Sam. 25:1-44) is a superb example of negotiation. As David's army threatens Nabal for failing to provide food as requested, Nabal's wife, Abigail, shrewdly brings food and intercepts David before he can attack. She appeals to his interest—his clean record and honorable reputation—which will be sullied if he stains his hands with innocent blood. Abigail's brilliant appeal brings him to his senses; he recants. Her tactic illustrates a key principle in cooperative negotiation: the more fully you understand your opponent's interests, the more persuasive and effective you can be in negotiating an agreement.

4. Search for creative solutions

Seek solutions that will satisfy as many interests as possible. Begin by spontaneously mentioning any idea that springs to mind. Encourage imagination and creativity; postpone evaluating and deciding. The best solution may involve combining several options.

Try to "expand the pie", bringing in additional interests that could be satisfied as part of your agreement so everyone can benefit more. If the primary issue is whether your neighbor will replace his broken fence, you might offer to help him remove some diseased trees that threaten to fall on your garage.

As you focus on solutions that seem wise to you, explain how these solutions benefit your opponent. By focusing on shared interests and developing options that benefit everyone, you create incentives for parties to agree on more difficult points of contention.

5. Evaluate options objectively and reasonably
Even if the previous steps have gone well, this stage may bring on differences of opinion. Try to be objective as you evaluate your options. (Allowing things to degenerate into a battle of subjective opinions will waste your previous good work.) Introduce facts, rules and regulations, or professional reports, or seek respected advice.

The book of Daniel illustrates an objective evaluation. An official, afraid of punishment, refuses to allow Daniel to eat different food than the ceremonially unclean food and wine he is offered in the king's service. Daniel wisely negotiates (Dan. 1:11-16) a proposal that honors everyone's interests: by testing Daniel and his friends for 10 days by serving only vegetables and water, the official ideally will see that they remain healthy and well-nourished. When the 10-day test shows that Daniel's solution was valid, a permanent agreement was quickly reached.

Besides using objective criteria, try to discern the hidden reasons behind objections. Continue to put yourself in the other person's shoes. Build on the other person's ideas and words.

To avoid misunderstandings, try to put in writing any agreement reached. Include what issues were resolved, actions to take, who is responsible for what, deadline dates, and how results will be evaluated.

During the Session

Introductory time (10 mins.)
1. Begin on time. Ask members to relate any new prayer requests and to update the group on answered prayer. As you begin the prayer time, review prayer requests offered and call for volunteers to pray for items mentioned. As

leader close the prayer time. In your prayer mention any requests that have not been prayed over.

2. For the opening activity, direct members to item 1 of week 4 in the *Member Book*. Ask members to read the statements in item 1 and put a star by the one which typifies how they feel about others' interests.

Group discussion (35 mins.)

3. Give a two-minute, general summation of cooperative versus competitive negotiation, based on the material in the sections "Material Issues" and "Cooperative v. Competitive Negotiation." Avoid mentioning specific pros and cons of each type of negotiation. Based on what you have explained, direct members to item 2 in the *Member Book*. Ask them to list what they believe are advantages and disadvantages to each type of negotiating. For example, tell members that a "pro" of competitive negotiating is that people could say exactly what they feel like saying to their opponents and leave feeling as though they had gotten everything off their chests. A disadvantage to that style is that people might lose friends in the process and destroy any opportunity for productive problem-solving.

4. Give a one-minute summation of "Prepare" in the PAUSE Process. Using the flip-chart list that you made in advance, highlight each of the activities that are included in the "Prepare" step. Note how this step alone contrasts with some styles of competitive negotiating just mentioned—especially the type of negotiating in which one person lashes out angrily at his or her opponent. Ask members to turn to item 3 in the *Member Book* and write their response to the following statement: "You can either put your time into grumbling about a problem or put that time into carefully negotiating with others. The sooner you devote your time to finding a solution to the problem, the less time you will spend stewing over it." After giving them two minutes to write their answers, ask a volunteer to share his or her thoughts on that statement.

5. Give a one-minute summation of "Affirm relation-ships" in the PAUSE Process. Using the flip chart list that you made in advance, highlight each of the ways to affirm relationships that are included in this step. Ask members to turn to item 4 in the *Member Book*. Ask them to describe a time they can recall when they affirmed a relationship as they began to discuss a conflict situation. Tell them to include how it impacted the outcome of the negotiations. After members have had about a minute to write their answers, call for a volunteer to say what he or she wrote down. You may want to share your own experi-ence, such as, *My husband's parents, who are divorced from each other, both wanted to spend Christmas this year with our children. My husband's father always waits until the last minute to make his plans and then feels slighted when we can't seem to make time for him. In trying to negotiate a solution, I first thanked Grandfather for caring about our kids and for always remembering them at Christmas with a generous money gift. This affirmation seemed to make him more willing to listen.*

6. Give a two-minute summation of the next two steps in the PAUSE process, "Understand interests" and "Search for creative solutions." Based on what you have told them about issues, positions, and interests, have them fill in the blanks in item 5 in the *Member Book*. Make brief note of the David, Nabal, and Abigail story and mention that members wanting to further study this insightful biblical illustration of understanding interests may do so in the "For Further Study" portion of their lesson.

7. Give a one-minute overview of the final PAUSE step, "Evaluate options objectively and reasonably." As you summarize, avoid referring to specifics of the Daniel story except to say that the Daniel story is an out-standing example of an objective evaluation. Then ask members to turn to item 6 in the *Member Book*. Ask them to read the Daniel story in their Bibles (Dan. 1:11-16). Then ask them to answer questions under item 6: What was the issue in this conflict? *Whether Daniel would eat the*

king's food and defile himself. What were the king's probable interests? *To have healthy, productive workers.* What were his officials' probable interests? *To obey the king and keep their heads.* What were Daniel's interests? *To obey and honor God and stay alive.* How did Daniel objectively evaluate a possible solution? *He respectfully suggested a brief, trial run on a different diet. Afterward the official could evaluate the results.)*

9. (optional, if time allows) Show Peacemaker Parable "Word Pictures" (9 mins.). Acknowledge that members have already seen this parable, but ask them to view it this time with an eye toward identifying negotiations techniques. Ask members to answer these questions in item 7 in the *Member Book* as they view the brief parable: What issue is the couple negotiating? Is it competitive or cooperative negotiation? *Janet is attempting to negotiate a way to get Jim to open up to her so she can feel close to him as she once did. It begins as competitive negotiation but has some elements of cooperative negotiation after Janet begins using her strategy.* What about the couple's interaction indicates that Janet prepared for her negotiation with Jim? *Instead of merely accusing, Janet prepares a series of word pictures to help Jim see how he has moved from being open with her to being closed as though he were in a prison. Janet thinks that this, along with the James Taylor illustration, will help Jim understand how she feels.* In a true cooperative negotiation situation, what interests of Jim's would Janet have attempted to understand? *She would have affirmed him for his diligent work at the office and his determination to provide for the family. She would have understood what a grave impact Jim's past job loss had on his sense of self.*

Preview further study (1 min.)

10. Direct members to item 8 in the *Member Book* regarding optional further study. Explain that this week's extra work involves reading from *The Peacemaker*, reading the five daily devotionals (adapted from *The Peacemaker*),

completing the study "Focusing on Interests: The Wisdom
of Abigail", and completing "If You Are Presently
Involved in a Conflict."

Closure (4 mins.)
11. Thank members for their participation. Remind them
that you will pray for them during the week. Encourage
them to pray for each other as the Lord brings other members to mind.
12. In closing, ask members to think about one way they
have experienced God working in their lives to change
the way they view conflict. Call on a couple of volunteers
to share. As leader close in prayer. Ask God to keep the
members open to ways He would have them react differently in conflict situations.

After the Session

1. Pray for members. This is the best support you can give
them as they seek to learn to become peacemakers. Begin
praying for members' continued growth after this study
ends in two more sessions. Ask God to continue to work
in their hearts as they apply these concepts.
2. Continue to evaluate your leadership. Refer to the questions listed in earlier "After the Session" sections to
focus on your leadership abilities.
3. Read "Before the Session" for group session 5 to determine the amount of preparation you will need for the
next group session. At the top of the group session 5
material in this *Leader Guide*, record when you will do
your preparation.
4. Carefully study week 6 and complete all the exercises to
stay ahead of the group.

Overcome Evil with Good

GROUP SESSION 5

Before the Session

1. Review week 5. Read and complete the lesson for week 6 to stay ahead of the group.
2. Master this week's material in the *Leader Guide*.
3. If you are using the video or DVD, arrange for a VCR or DVD player and a monitor during the session.
4. Using a flip chart and a marker, prepare for part of the discussion by writing on a sheet of the flip chart a list containing the following principles: Control Your Tongue, Seek Godly Advisers, Do What Is Right, Recognize Your Limits, and Use the Ultimate Weapon. You will use this as part of item 3 in the *Member Book*.
5. The next two sessions are crucial in terms of leaving members inspired and equipped to continue their peacemaking activities. Ask God to help you as you endeavor to leave members committed to the peacemaking lifestyle.
6. Plan to stay within the given times for each activity.

The Lesson
By Ken Sande
Author of *The Peacemaker*

Using Divine Weapons

Peacemaking does not always go as easily as we desire. Although some people will make peace readily, others will be stubborn and defensive and will resist our reconciliation efforts. Sometimes they will become even more antagonistic and will find new ways to frustrate or mistreat us. Our natural reaction is to strike back at people or to stop doing anything good to them. As this study has revealed, however, Jesus calls us to take a remarkably different course of action (see Luke 6:27-28).

From a wordly perspective, this approach seems naive and appears to concede defeat, but the apostle Paul knew better. He had learned that God's ways are not the world's ways. He also understood the profound power we have through Christ. When he was subjected to intense and repeated personal attacks, he used the words of 2 Corinthians 10:3-5 to describe his response.

Paul realized that a true peacemaker's identity in Christ guides, motivates, and empowers him or her. This identity is based on faith in the most amazing promise we could ever hear: God has forgiven all our sins and made peace with us through His Son's death and resurrection.

Consequently He has given us the freedom and power to turn from sin (and conflict), to be conformed to the likeness of Christ, and to be His ambassadors of reconciliation (2 Cor. 5:16-20).

Realizing who we are in Christ inspires us to do the unnatural work of dying to self, confessing sin, addressing others' wrongs graciously, laying down our rights, and forgiving deep hurts—even with people who persist in opposing or mistreating us.

Paul also understood that God has given us divine weapons for our quest for peace: Scripture, prayer, truth, righteousness, the gospel, faith, love, joy, peace, patience, kindness, goodness, gentleness, and self-control (Eph. 6:10-18; Gal. 5:22-23). Many people regard these resources and qualities as feeble and useless when dealing with "real" problems. Yet these are the very weapons that Jesus used to defeat Satan and to conquer the world! (see Matt. 4:1-11; 11:28-30; John 14:15-17) Since Jesus chose to use these weapons instead of resorting to worldly weapons,

But I tell you who hear me: Love your enemies, do good to those who hate you, bless those who curse you, pray for those who mistreat you (Luke 6:27-28).

For though we live in the world, we do not wage war as the world does. The weapons we fight with are not the weapons of the world. On the contrary, they have divine power to demolish strongholds. We demolish arguments and every pretension that sets itself up against the knowledge of God, and we take captive every thought and make it obedient to Christ (2 Cor. 10:3-5).

we are to do the same. Romans 12:14-21 tells us how to behave as we wield these spiritual weapons, especially when dealing with people who oppose or mistreat us.

Paul understood the classic military principle that the best defense is an effective offense. He did not tell us to be passive against evil but to go on the offensive—not to ignore, beat down, or destroy our opponents but to win them over, to help them see the truth, and to bring them into a right relationship with God.

As Romans 12:14-21 indicates, five basic principles contribute to a victorious offensive. In previous chapters we have mentioned most of these principles. We now will re-examine them to see how we can use them with people who have persistently and stubbornly resisted our efforts to make peace.

Control Your Tongue

Bless those who persecute you; bless and do not curse (Rom. 12:14).

Controlling your tongue grows more important as the conflict intensifies (see Rom. 12:14). In prolonged conflict, you may be sorely tempted to indulge in gossip, slander, and reckless words, especially if your opponent says critical things about you. But if you react with harsh words or gossip, you only worsen matters.

Do not repay evil with evil or insult with insult, but with blessing, because to this you were called so that you may inherit a blessing (1 Pet. 3:9).

Even if your opponent speaks maliciously against you or to you, do not respond in kind. Instead, make every effort to breathe grace by saying only what is both true and helpful. Speak well of your opponent whenever possible; use kind and gracious language. See what Peter says in 1 Peter 3:9 (see margin.)

Besides preventing further offenses, controlling your tongue can help you maintain a loving attitude and an accurate perspective of your situation. Hence, you likely will think and behave more wisely and constructively than you would if you indulged in all kinds of critical talk. Instead of undermining further progress, you will be prepared to take advantage of new opportunities for dialogue and negotiation.

Seek Godly Advisers

As Paul says (see Rom. 12:15-16), battling evil alone is difficult. This is why developing relationships with wise and encouraging people who will give you sound biblical advice is important. These friends also can correct and admonish you when they see you erring (see Prov. 27:5-6).

Godly advisers help especially when you are involved in a difficult conflict and don't see the results you desire. If a lack of noticeable progress causes you to doubt biblical principles, you may be tempted to abandon God's ways and to resort to the world's tactics. One of the best ways to avoid straying from the Lord is to surround yourself with wise and spiritually mature people who encourage you to stay on a biblical course, even when the going is tough.

Keep Doing What Is Right

Paul also calls us to continue doing what is right even when we think our opponent will never cooperate (see Rom. 12:17). Paul did not mean that we become slaves to others' opinions. The Greek word that is translated "be careful" (*pronoeo*) means to give thought to the future, to plan in advance, or to take careful precaution. Therefore, Romans 12:17 means you are to plan and act so carefully and properly that any reasonable person who watches you eventually will acknowledge that what you did was right. Peter echoes the same principle in 1 Peter 2:12, 15, 3:15b-16.

1 Samuel 24:1-22 dramatically illustrates this principle. When King Saul—intending to murder David—pursued him relentlessly through the desert, Saul entered a cave in which David and his men hid. David's men urged him to kill the king, but David refused (see 1 Sam. 24:10b). After Saul left the cave and walked away, David called after him. Read 1 Sam. 24:17-20 to see what the king told David.

Rejoice with those who rejoice; mourn with those who mourn. Live in harmony with one another. Do not be proud, but be willing to associate with people of low position. Do not be conceited (Rom. 12:15-16).

Better is open rebuke than hidden love. Wounds from a friend can be trusted, but an enemy multiplies kisses (Prov. 27:5-6).

Do not repay evil for evil. Be careful to do what is right in the eyes of everybody (Rom. 12:17).

Some urged me to kill you, but I spared you; I said, "I will not lift my hand against my master, because he is the Lord's anointed" (1 Sam. 24:10b).

Years later, Saul's prediction came true—David ascended the throne of Israel. David's determination to obey God and to keep doing what was right helped him to avoid saying and doing things he later would have regretted. As a result, all of his enemies eventually were won over or defeated. Thousands of years later people still take note of David's righteousness.

Recognize Your Limits

If it is possible, as far as it depends on you, live at peace with everyone (Rom. 12:18).

Know your limits when you deal with difficult people. Even when you continue to do what is right, some people may adamantly refuse to live at peace with you. See what Paul says in Romans 12:18. You cannot force others to do what is right. If you have done everything within your power to resolve a conflict, you have fulfilled your responsibility to God and may stop actively trying to solve the problem. If circumstances change and you have new opportunities to seek peace with an opponent, do so. Meanwhile, avoid wasting time, energy, and resources fretting about someone who refuses to be reconciled.

Accepting your limits is easier if you have a biblical view of success. The world defines success in terms of what a person possesses, controls, or accomplishes. God defines success in terms of faithful obedience to His will. The world asks, "What results have you achieved?" God asks, "Were you faithful to my ways?" The Lord controls the ultimate outcome of all you do. He knows that even your best efforts will not always accomplish what you desire. This is why He does not hold you accountable for

Fear God and keep his commandments, for this is the whole duty of man (Eccl. 12:13b).

specific results. Instead, he asks for only one thing—obedience to His revealed will (see Eccl. 12:13b). If you have done all that you can to be reconciled to someone, you have fulfilled your duty and are a success in God's eyes. Let Him take things from there.

This realization will help you to resist the temptation to take personal revenge on someone who is doing wrong. Don't even dream about it! Paul reminds us that God is responsible for punishing those who do not repent (see Rom. 12:19 and Prov. 20:22). God has many instruments that he can use to bring evil people to justice and deliver you from them. Among other things, he can use the church (Matt. 18:17-20), the civil courts (Rom. 13:1-5), or even Satan (1 Cor. 5:5) to deal with unrepentant people.

Wait for God to deal with people in his own way (Pss. 37 and 73). Although His results may occur more slowly than you desire, they always will be better than anything you could bring about on your own.

Use the Ultimate Weapon

The ultimate weapon for responding to a stubborn opponent is *deliberate, focused love* (see Rom. 12:20-21). Instead of reacting spitefully to those who mistreat you, Jesus wants you to discern their deepest needs and do all you can to meet those needs. Sometimes this will require going to them to show them their faults. At other times they may need mercy, compassion, patience, and words of encouragement. You even may have opportunities to provide material and financial assistance to those who least deserve it or expect it from you.

Paul's reference to "burning coals on his head" indicates the irresistible power of deliberate, focused love. Ancient armies often used burning coals to fend off attackers (see Ps. 120:4). No soldier could resist this weapon for long; eventually it would overcome even the most determined attacker. Love has the same irresistible power. At the very least, actively loving an enemy will protect you from being spiritually defeated by anger, bitterness, and a thirst for revenge. And in some cases, God may use your active and determined love for your opponent to bring that person to repentance.

Do not take revenge, my friends, but leave room for God's wrath, for it is written: "It is mine to avenge; I will repay," says the Lord (Rom. 12:19).

Do not say, "I'll pay you back for this wrong!" Wait for the Lord, and he will deliver you (Prov. 20:22).

If your enemy is hungry, feed him; if he is thirsty, give him something to drink. In doing this, you will heap burning coals on his head (Rom. 12:20-21).

He will punish you with a warrior's sharp arrows, with burning coals of the broom tree (Ps. 120:4).

During the Session

Introductory time (10 mins.)

1. Greet members as they arrive. Begin on time even if not all class members are present. Welcome any who might just now be joining the group for the first time. Since your group has open membership, having participants who join even as the study ends is not uncommon. Make certain they feel welcome even at this point in the study. Make the *Member Book* available to them.

2. As an opening exercise, ask members to turn to item 1 in the *Member Book*. Ask them to complete the statement: "At this point in the study, my largest, ongoing challenge in being a peacemaker is . . .." As leader first share your own response to this question. You might say something such as, *Praying for those who hurt me and asking God to bless them continues to be the most difficult thing for me to do as a peacemaker.* Give members one minute to write their answers to item 1. Then call on a volunteer willing to share his or her answer.

3. Begin with a time of prayer. Ask one or two volunteers to pray for some of the matters just discussed. Suggest that they ask God to help each person with the challenge they cited in item 1.

Group discussion (35 mins.)

4. Give a two-minute, general summation of the lesson section "Using Divine Weapons." (For purposes of the members' upcoming exercise in the *Member Book*, leave out direct references to the Scripture passages listed in item 2. They will turn their attention to these momentarily.) Direct members to item 2 in the *Member Book*. Ask them to take about five minutes to look up the Scripture passages in the left-hand column. Ask them to write in the right-hand column one divine weapon that the passage mentions that we have as Christians to use (as opposed to the ways the world offers in our quest for

peace. (Answers: *Luke 6:27-28, 35-36; prayer; 2 Cor. 10:5, taking thoughts captive; 2 Cor. 5:18, the ministry of reconciliation; Gal. 5:22-23, the fruit of the Spirit; Rom. 12:14, blessing; John 14:15-17, the Holy Spirit.*)

5. Tell members that one of the most important points that they will hear in this entire study is contained in the section of *The Peacemaker* that you just highlighted. Read to members the second, third, and fourth full paragraphs on page 121. As you read the fourth paragraph, ask them to turn to item 3 in the *Member Book* and fill in the blanks as you read. Tell them you trust they will remember these statements long after the study is finished.

6. Give a seven- to eight-minute summation of the five basic principles contributing to a victorious offensive: Control Your Tongue, Seek Godly Advisers, Do What Is Right, Recognize Your Limits, and Use the Ultimate Weapon. As you speak, direct members' attention to the flip chart on which you have listed these five principles and ask them to write the five basic principles in item 4. Direct members to item 5 in the *Member Book*. Ask them to read the five vignettes and decide which of the five principles is being used in each case study. (Answers: *1. Control Your Tongue; 2. Use the Ultimate Weapon; 3. Seek Godly Advisers; 4. Recognize Your Limits; 5. Keep Doing What Is Right).* Give members about five minutes to work on the activity. Then ask them to call out the answers.

7. Ask members to discuss which of the five principles they find most difficult to enact in their lives. Conduct a five-minute discussion on the pros and cons of the various principles.

8. (optional, if time allows) Show Peacemaker Parable "Why Not Rather Be Wronged?" (4 mins.). Ask members to answer these questions in item 6 in the *Member Book* as they view the brief parable: Which of the five godly principles discussed in this lesson was Scott following in dealing with the lawsuit? *Do What Is Right; also, Use the Ultimate Weapon.* Why did his attorney fail to understand when Scott spoke of wanting a clean conscience? *The*

*attorney was responding to conflict in terms of the world's ways
by insisting that they pursue the lawsuit to extract damages.*
What word picture did Scott paint in talking about his
outlook on dropping the case? *He spoke about the Judge who
allowed his innocent son to die to pay for the wrongs of both
Scott and Hooverman, who, as brothers, were both guilty co-
conspirators.* How difficult would taking a costly stand, as
Scott did, be for you? Why? *Your answer.*

Preview further study (1 min.)

9. Direct members to item 7 in the *Member Book* regarding
optional further study. Explain that the extra work for this
week involves reading from *The Peacemaker*, reading the
five daily devotionals (adapted from *The Peacemaker*), and
completing "If You Are Presently Involved in a Conflict."

Closure (4 mins.)

10. Tell members that they may be feeling a bit sad as the
time in this group study draws to a close. Note that they
may have found beneficial the type of sharing that occurs
in a study of this nature, in which members talk about
difficult circumstances in their lives and learn that others
have walked similar paths. Encourage them all to continue in a Sunday-school class or to join a small-group Bible
study, where this type of bonding may continue.
11. In closing, ask members to pair up for prayer time.
Ask them to each thank God for something that they have
learned during today's session or some positive
growth experience that has occurred from this *Peacefakers,
Peacebreakers, and Peacemakers* study.

After the Session

1. Thank God for each person He has brought to
your study. Pray that the time invested in this topic will
make a difference throughout his or her life. Pray particularly for your final session together.

2. Look into other courses that your group might use as a follow-up to *Peacefakers, Peacebreakers, and Peacemakers,* if the church has not offered these already. Possibilities include *The Peacemaker Seminar* to help members reinforce what they learned in *Peacefakers, Peacebreakers, and Peacemakers.* Other possibilities include *PeaceSowers, Guiding People through Conflict,* and the *Reconciler Training Course.* Determine whether any of these is right for your group. Options include beginning a new study immediately, taking a two-week break between studies, or beginning a new study during the summer or after the Christmas holidays. If you plan to broach this subject with your group, prepare to give a brief synopsis of the study or studies you are considering. Plan how you will order materials if the group decides to move forward quickly on another peacemaking study.

3. Read "Before the Session" for group session 6 to determine the amount of preparation you will need for the next group session. At the top of the group session 6 material in this *Leader Guide,* record when you will do your preparation.

Cultivating a Culture of Peace in Your Church

GROUP SESSION 6

Before the Session

1. Review week 6.
2. Master this week's material in the *Leader Guide.*
3. If you are using the video or DVD, arrange for a VCR or DVD player and a monitor during the session.
4. This lesson mentions several additional resources that churches may use to further members' knowledge of peacemaking. If you have not done so already, acquaint yourself with *Guiding People through Conflict, Transforming Your Church,* and *The Young Peacemaker* so you can speak knowledgeably about them in your lesson.
5. Prepare a flip chart and a marker so you will be prepared if your group decides to develop an action plan for steps it may feel led to take to further the peacemaking process at your church. As members brainstorm ideas, you may write them on the flip chart.
6. Using a flip chart and a marker, prepare a list containing the five levels of a peacemaking culture: Level 1: a culture of disbelief; Level 2: a culture of faith; Level 3: a culture of transformation; Level 4: a culture of peace; Level 5: a culture of multiplication. You will use this with item 3 in the *Member Book.*
7. Prepare eight slips of paper. Each piece will contain a Scripture verse that accompanies one the eight traits of a peacemaking church (look at pp. 134-135 for information to use in preparing the slips of paper.) You will use this with item 4 in the *Member Book.*

8. Again using the flip chart, write a list containing the following eight traits of a peacemaking church: vision, training, assistance, perseverance, accountability, restoration, stability, witness. You will also use this as part of item 4 in the *Member Book*.

9. If you plan to discuss with members possible follow-up studies to *Peacefakers, Peacebreakers, and Peacemakers,* bring copies of the resources you are considering so you can show the workbooks to members as you discuss the options.

10. Pray for each group member. Ask God to help members be blessings to those around them as a result of what they have learned during the group study. Ask Him to help you lead effectively during this concluding session.

11. Plan to stay within the given times for each activity.

The Lesson

By Ken Sande
Author of *The Peacemaker*

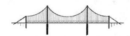

A Culture of Peace

Churches everywhere are changing how they respond to conflict. By God's grace they are deliberately training their congregations to make peace. As they develop a "culture of peace", they are discovering the wonderful blessing promised by James 3:18 (see the margin).

Peacemakers who sow in peace raise a harvest of righteousness (Jas. 3:18).

This harvest James mentions involves a wide variety of relational fruit. When a local church teaches its people to live out the gospel in the conflicts of daily life, people are more willing to admit their shortcomings and to seek help before a crisis occurs. Families deal with disputes better. This makes divorce less likely. Members are encouraged to go to each other to discuss problems instead of letting issues fester. Church growth improves, since the church is protected from division and splits; offended members are less likely to leave.

Pastors and other church leaders benefit as well. When leaders fulfill their shepherding responsibilities more fully, respect and appreciation for their work grows. As they are taken out of the day-to-day "complaint loop", they can spend less time dealing with disgruntled members and more time on forward-moving ministry. When members learn to stop gossiping, leaders are subjected to less criticism. As conflict declines, stress on church leaders' families often is reduced. When respectful discussion and reconciliation are the norm, pastors and other leaders are less likely to burn out or be forced out of their jobs.

They had such a sharp disagreement that they parted company (Acts 15:39).

Of course, no church sees all these benefits at once. Our sin continually works against a culture of peace. Even Paul and Barnabas had a falling out! (see Acts 15:39) Don't be surprised when members forget what they have learned, leaders are inconsistent, and our efforts seem in vain. Although we stumble, we need not fall, for the Lord upholds us (see Ps. 37:24). As He helps us back to our feet, we can learn from our mistakes, forgive each other, and continue to grow.

Though he stumble, he will not fall, for the Lord upholds him with his hand (Ps. 37:24).

Resolving conflicts biblically also enhances outreach and evangelism. In a fallen world conflict is inevitable. When unsaved people see Christians admitting their failures and forgiving and reconciling, they cannot help but notice. The more our relationships reflect God's mercy and love, the more people will want to know about the Power in us. What a great way to increase the harvest!

Leading a Cultural Transformation

A few years ago most of these peacemaking churches had anything but a culture of peace. Instead, a *culture of disbelief* reigned. They did not believe they could do much to help their members deal with conflict. They did not really understand what the Bible teaches about peacemaking. They lacked faith that biblical principles actually would work in today's culture.

This disbelief robbed them of the ability to respond constructively and helpfully. They did not provide their members with any practical helps for personal conflict resolution. Gossip, broken relationships, divorce, and steady member turnover characterized their churches. They also lost much of their ability to be effective witnesses to Jesus Christ's reconciling love and forgiveness.

God graciously led these church leaders to look honestly at their "peacemaking culture"—the combination of *attitudes, traditions, habits, and abilities for resolving conflict.* What they saw troubled them. They realized that their church cultures did not promote peacemaking. They asked God to help them change.

Pastors played a key role in transforming their churches. Their preaching and personal example set the stage for change, while they wisely delegated most of the day-to-day educational and reconciliation work to elders and other gifted people in the congregation. Together, they transformed their church culture and steadily raised their level of peacemaking productivity. This transformation typically involves five levels of growth.

Level 1—A Culture of Disbelief: People lack practical training in resolving conflict. They doubt that the church can help them resolve their differences. This church is like a tree missing some of its sweetest fruit.

Level 2—A Culture of Faith: People begin to understand God's peacemaking commands and promises and to believe that His ways will work in today's culture. This church is like a tree blossoming in the spring.

Level 3—A Culture of Transformation: People want to put off worldly ways of resolving conflict and take steps to learn how to respond to conflict biblically. This church is like a tree being pruned and cultivated for greater productivity.

Level 4—A Culture of Peace: People are eager and able to resolve conflict and reconcile relationships in a way that clearly reflects the love and power of Jesus Christ. This church is like a tree producing a rich harvest.

Level 5—A Culture of Multiplication: People delight in expanding God's kingdom by showing other people and churches how they, too, can be peacemakers. This church is like a tree that reproduces itself by spreading its seed.

Characteristics of a Culture of Peace

A church that has a culture of peace usually has eight essential traits:

- **Vision**—This church is eager to bring glory to God by demonstrating the reconciling love and forgiveness of Jesus Christ. It sees peacemaking as an essential part of the Christian life (Luke 6:27-36; John 13:35; 1 Cor. 10:31; Col. 3:12-14).
- **Training**—The church knows that peacemaking does not occur naturally, so it deliberately trains both its leaders and its members to respond to conflict biblically in all areas of life (Gal. 5:19-21; Luke 6:40; Eph. 4:24-26; 1 Tim. 4:15-16; Titus 2:1-10).
- **Assistance**—When members cannot resolve disputes privately, the church assists them through in-house, trained reconcilers, even when conflicts involve financial, employment, or legal issues (Matt. 18:16; Rom. 15:14; 1 Cor. 6:1-8; Gal. 6:1-2; Col. 3:16).
- **Perseverance**—Just as God pursues us, the church works diligently to restore broken relationships, especially when a marriage is at stake, and even when attorneys are involved (Matt. 18:12-16; 19:1-9; Rom. 12:18; Eph. 4:1-3; 19:1-9; 1 Cor. 7:1-11).
- **Accountability**—If members refuse to listen to private correction, church leaders get directly involved to hold members accountable to Scripture and to promote repentance, justice, and forgiveness (Prov. 3:11-12; Matt. 18:15-20; 1 Cor. 5:1-5; Jas. 5:19-20).
- **Restoration**—Wanting to imitate God's amazing mercy and grace, the church gladly forgives and fully restores members who have genuinely repented of

serious and embarrassing sins (Matt. 18:21-35;
Eph. 4:32; 2 Cor. 2:5-11).
* **Stability**—Because relationships are valued and protected, leaders serve fruitfully year after year, and
members see the church as their long-term home
(1 Tim. 4:15; Heb. 10:25).
* **Witness**—Members are equipped and encouraged to
practice peacemaking so openly in their daily lives
that others will notice, ask why they do it, and hear
about the love of Christ (Matt. 5:9; John 13:34-35;
17:20-23; 1 Pet. 2:12; 3:15-16).

How to Transform a Church Culture

Peacemaking is an attitude expressed through action.
Jesus died on the cross to release us from the penalty of
sin. He gave His life to buy our forgiveness, earn our freedom, and bring us back to God. Now He wants us to pass
this gift of reconciliation on to others in the form of personal peacemaking (see Col. 3:12-13).

Therefore, as God's chosen people, holy and dearly loved, clothe yourselves with compassion, kindness, humility, gentleness and patience. Bear with each other and forgive whatever grievances you may have against one another (Col. 3:12-13).

These attitudes and actions do not spring naturally
from us. Therefore, in order to build a culture of peace, a
church must help its people both to put off worldly ways
for resolving conflict and to put on peacemaking attitudes
and actions that mirror our reconciliation with God.

This requires a lot of work. Senior pastors do not have
time to resolve everybody's battles. They may educate
from the pulpit and sometimes may aid in difficult conflicts, but typically they can entrust most of these activities to capable congregation leaders and members. (Refer
to the advice that Moses received when he tired from
serving as sole judge of Israel—Ex. 18:18-23.)

Cultivating a culture of peace involves five activities:

1. Gaining support from church leadership. Although
God often works through the church's laity to begin interest in peacemaking, cultural transformation will occur
only when church leaders officially support and lead this
effort. Most ideal is when a senior pastor views peace-

making not as a helpful side ministry but as something vital to the church's well-being and fruitfulness.

2. Forming a core support group (sometimes known as a Church Reconciler Team—including church leaders and laypeople)—responsible for guiding educational and reconciliation activities within the church.

3. Educating the entire congregation in peacemaking. Do this through two stages: a preaching series that raises the congregation's awareness about peacemaking, followed by each person's participation in a small-group Bible study or Sunday-school class to learn specific peacemaking principles and how to apply them.

4. Training gifted people within your congregation to become reconcilers. These trained church members or leaders may be conflict coaches (advising one person how to respond to conflict biblically) or mediators (meeting with both parties to facilitate discussion and agreement). These reconcilers can provide counsel and assistance in personal, family, employment, business, and even legal disputes.

5. Upgrading your church's organizational documents to support peacemaking and reduce legal liability. Churches are being sued—with costly judgments resulting—for negligence, breach of confidentiality, defamation, sexual misconduct, and intentional infliction of emotional distress. Church leaders sometimes are held personally responsible. Upgrade church bylaws and adopt special policies for counseling confidentiality, conflict resolution, and church discipline to reduce exposure to legal liability. (Contact Peacemaker Ministries for model documents.)

Some churches can make substantial progress in all areas within two years, while others take four or five years. Even small efforts produce noticeable fruit. A few people going through a Sunday-school class on peacemaking, such as this one, can have a ripple effect on their own families and friends. As members share with others what they learn and as relationships improve, an interest in peacemaking can grow.

The "Level-5 Church"—a Culture of Multiplication

Great responsibility accompanies our blessings. God has blessed the church with the gift of peacemaking in a conflicted world, but many churches do not use this talent. One day God will hold them accountable (see Matt. 25:24-27). Ask God to help you build a culture of peace that is so fruitful that it overflows into your community, other churches, and your denomination. Many churches are already doing this in these ways:

1. Equipping members to carry peacemaking into everyday life. As people see church members interact with others in a peacemaking way, they may seek them out for advice. This opens the way to invite others to church. When a church is known for resolving "small" problems, it will have greater credibility when it speaks to "large" issues impacting an entire community.

2. Teaching peacemaking to children. *The Young Peacemaker* can be taught in Sunday school or vacation Bible-school classes advertised to people outside the church. As children and parents benefit from this training, they may be drawn to the church and to the Lord.

3. Sending peacemakers on mission teams. By implementing conflict-resolution skills, these persons can help protect teams from destructive internal conflict and from conflicts on the field. They can also teach these skills to pastors in other countries.

4. Developing a church-based reconciliation ministry. Your church reconcilers can make their services available to people outside your church. This practical ministry demonstrates the gospel's power to unchurched or unsaved people who are in conflict. It can draw them to your church as it helps them make peace.

5. Sharing your experience with other churches in your community or denomination. Host a *Peacemaker Seminar* in your community, or train your reconcilers to assist neighboring churches when they cannot resolve internal conflicts on their own.

Then the man who had received the one talent came. "Master", he said, "I knew that you are a hard man, harvesting where you have not sown and gathering where you have not scattered seed. So I was afraid and went out and hid your talent in the ground. See, here is what belongs to you." His master replied, "You wicked, lazy servant! So you knew that I harvest where I have not sown and gather where I have not scattered seed? Well then, you should have put my money on deposit with the bankers, so that when I returned I could have received it back with interest" (Matt. 25:24-27).

6. Planting new churches that have peacemaking as part of their original "DNA." Pass on the spiritual trait of peacemaking as your church plants new congregations. This gift will increase the new church's ability to survive natural growing pains and thrive as a family of believers.

Start Today with You

The only thing necessary is for one person to hear the call of God and respond, "Here am I. Send me!" (Isa. 6:8). Perhaps that person is you. Ask God to give you a longing to see a culture of peace in your church that reflects the love and power of His Son. If He gives you that longing, diligent work awaits you, but great blessing is also in store. Jesus' promise in Matthew 5 is dependable: "Blessed are the peacemakers, for they will be called the sons of God" (v. 9).

During the Session

Introductory time (10 mins.)

1. Welcome each member. Beginning on time, thank members for their faithful participation in the *Peacefakers, Peacebreakers, and Peacemakers* study. Assure them that you will continue to be available to them to discuss questions that they might have as a result of this study.

2. Ask each member to state one thing he or she has grown to appreciate about the member seated on his or her right as the group has participated in the study. As leader begin by telling one thing you have grown to appreciate about the member on your right. If you condense your reply and answer in about 45 seconds, other members are more likely to follow suit. Go around the room until each member has had a turn. Because of the open nature of the group, you possibly may have a group member who, on this last day of the study, is attending for

the first time. Suggest that any member who does not
know well the person on his or her right simply say, "God
bless you", and move the process on to the next person.
3. As leader open the session in prayer. Thank God for
the traits and instances of growth to which members have
just alluded. Thank Him for how He has been present
during the past weeks of study and how He has stirred
members to think of peacemaking in a different light.

Group discussion (35 mins.)

4. Ask members to turn to item 1 of week 6 in their
Member Book. Note to members that in previous weeks the
group has studied about some of the personal benefits of
the peacemaking process. Explain that in today's concluding lesson they will look at how a church, as a whole, can
benefit from cultivating a culture of peace. Without your
giving any further information at this point, ask them to
list in item 1 four benefits that spring to their minds about
ways a *church* would benefit from its members becoming
peacemakers, or cultivating "a culture of peace." After
giving members about two minutes to write their
answers, call for the group members to discuss their
answers for about five minutes. Then give a one-minute
summary of the section "A Culture of Peace."
5. Direct members to item 2 in the *Member Book*. Ask
members to fill in the blanks in the definition of a "culture
of peace", based on the one-minute summary you just
gave them. If you need to refresh their memories, read for
them the definition of a "peacemaking culture" found on
page 133 of this book. Ask them to supply the correct
words in the blanks of their definition.
6. Give a five-minute summation of the section "Leading
a Cultural Transformation." Using the flip-chart list you
prepared in advance, describe the various levels, pointing
to each on the flip chart as you describe it. Direct members to item 3 in the *Member Book*. Tell members, "Based
on the levels you just heard described, put a check by the
level of peacemaking you believe your own church has

reached at this time." Then direct them to the second part of that question, "If you did not indicate that your church was at level 5, what do you think would be required for your church to reach a higher level?" Give members about one minute to write their answers. Tell them you will discuss their answers later in the session.

7. Tell members that a church that has a culture of peace usually has eight essential traits. Ask them to form eight groups. Some groups may contain only two members. If you do not have enough to form eight groups of two or more, you may need to allow an individual person to constitute a group for the upcoming assignment. Pass out the slips of paper you have already prepared that contain the groups of Scripture verses. Explain to members that each set of Scripture passages will lead them to one of the eight individual traits of a peacemaking church listed at the beginning of item 4. Ask each group to read its verses aloud to each other. With members collaborating, each group decides what trait the collection of verses is trying to describe. Give members about seven minutes to jointly decide which trait it represents. Then ask for group reports. After members have called out their answers, give a three-minute summary of the section, "Characteristics of a Culture of Peace" to see how close they came to finding the answers. To help them check their answers, use the flip-chart list you prepared in advance. Suggest that they write the answers for all eight traits as part of item 4 in the *Member Book*.

8. Direct members to item 5 in the *Member Book*. Ask them to write their personal answer to the question: Why is what Christ has done for you motivation to adopt a culture of peace? (They might answer something like this: *Because Jesus died on the cross to wipe away my sins and to forgive me, I want to exalt Him and follow His example and pass this gift of reconciliation on to others.*) Call on a volunteer to share his or her answer. Then give a five-minute summary of "How to Transform a Church Culture."

9. Direct members to item 6 in the *Member Book*. Ask each member to spend about two minutes prayerfully

writing an answer to the question, "What could your group do collectively to help bring about a culture of peace in your church?" Then lead a 10-minute brain-storming session with the group. Using the flip chart and marker, record answers as volunteers call out ways they answered item 6 in the *Member Book*. The action plan might contain suggestions such as the following: talk to the pastor and other church leaders about the need; offer to give testimonies in church about what members learned and how they benefited from the *Peacefakers, Peacebreakers, and Peacemakers* study; offer to train to be leaders of further *Peacefakers, Peacebreakers, and Peacemakers* classes; volunteer to assist in conflict situations; train to lead *The Young Peacemaker* in the children's area of the church. If the discussion seems to generate sufficient interest to warrant it, schedule an implementation of the plan. You might seek volunteers for various tasks mentioned and outline a time line for accomplishing them. For example, if one or two volunteers indicate they are willing to give testimonies in church, go with the momentum and establish a plan for getting these on the calendar. Explain to members briefly about further materials the group might study as a follow-up to *Peacefakers, Peacebreakers, and Peacemakers*. Determine whether the group would like to pursue a further study as part of its ongoing commitment to peacemaking.

10. Summarize in about two minutes the section "The 'Level-5 Church'—a Culture of Multiplication." Ask members whether the material you just outlined represented some new concepts for them. Ask whether they ever considered, for example, that your church might gain more credibility in the community when it speaks out on moral, ethical issues if it demonstrated a culture of peace among its membership. Remind members of the importance of "walking the walk" instead of merely "talking the talk" around unchurched persons and nonbelievers.

11. Conclude with a brief summary of the section "Start Today with You." Direct members to item 7 in the *Member Book*. Ask them to spend one minute writing their

response to the question about what they can do individually to help their church adopt a culture of peace. At the conclusion of your session you will ask them to pray a prayer that relates to what they wrote in this exercise.

12. (optional, if time allows) Show Peacemaker Parable "Peacemaker Junkie" (5 mins.). Ask members to answer these questions in item 8 in the *Member Book* as they view the brief parable: What underlying message does Ted attempt to convey as he checks in with the Peacemakers Anonymous group? *The vignette, a spoof on a support-group meeting in which members are "addicted" to peacemaking, attempts to convey how a person who tries biblical peacemaking efforts receives a "rush" of good feelings for doing what the Bible commands regarding making peace.* What did Ted really mean when he said he wanted to "live like a zombie again" and "get back to normal Christianity again"? *Although peacemaking can be exhilarating, it can be very intense, humbling, and difficult, all of which goes against our natural tendency to be lazy and selfish.*

Preview further study (1 min.)

13. Direct members to item 9 in the *Member Book* regarding optional further study. Explain that the extra work for this week involves reading from *The Peacemaker* and reading the five daily devotionals (adapted from *The Peacemaker*).

Closure (4 mins.)

14. Express your thanks to members for the privilege of leading them in this study. Reiterate your desire to remain available to them as needs arise or as they feel led to pursue peacemaking efforts.

15. Call members to a time of personal commitment as a result of what they answered during the class discussion and in item 6 in the *Member Book*. Ask them to pray silently, asking God to help them keep whatever commitments they might have made personally or as a group. As leader close the session in prayer.

After the Session

1. Thank God for giving you the strength and wisdom to lead this term of *Peacefakers, Peacebreakers, and Peacemakers*. Pray that each member will continue to benefit from the study and will be led to keep commitments made during the study, especially during the last session.
2. Evaluate your leadership of the group. Make notes on strengths and things you believe worked well with the group. Also list areas in which you desire to grow if you lead this study again.
3. If your group decided to pursue further study in one of the other resources on peacemaking, arrange to order necessary materials and make plans regarding scheduling and promoting the study.
4. Determine the areas in which you need to follow up with regard to decisions the group made for further action. Make appointments to visit with your pastor and church leaders, if necessary; arrange for testimonies to be given during worship; and take any other steps that might have been part of your group's action plan.

HOW TO FIND
NEW LIFE IN CHRIST

No matter who you are—what job you hold, how much (or how little) money you have, what you have achieved—you are powerless over one thing: going to heaven on your own strength. God is the power source for salvation to all who believe.

You need God's power because you, like the rest of us, are lost in sin. "For all have sinned and fall short of the glory of God" (Rom. 3:23).

A penalty exists for that sin. "For the wages of sin is death" (Rom. 6:23).

Good deeds cannot earn a way to wipe out that sin from your life. "For it is by grace you have been saved, through faith—and this is not from yourselves; it is the gift of God—not by works, so that no one can boast" (Eph. 2:8-9).

God provided for your sin when he sent His Son to die in your place. Instead of you, Jesus took the wages of sin on Himself by dying on the cross. "But God demonstrates his own love for us in this: While we were still sinners, Christ died for us" (Rom. 5:8). Then God raised Him on the third day.

You can claim this free gift of salvation by calling on Him. "Everyone who calls on the name of the Lord will be saved" (Rom. 10:13).

If you would like to have salvation in Jesus Christ, sincerely pray a prayer such as this one: "Dear God, I confess to You my sin and my need for salvation. I turn away from my sin and place my faith in Jesus as my Savior and Lord. Amen."

Now, find a pastor or Christian friend who you can tell about your decision.